◈ KEITH SUGDEN ◈

WALKING THE PILGRIM WAYS

PHOTOGRAPHS BY JOHN CLEARE

Illustrations by Clare Wake

*Parishioners abandoned these ruins in the Camarthenshire
countryside when they built themselves a more accessible
church in 1848. The name – Llanfihangel Abercowin –
describes their position on the old pilgrim route to St
David's: 'the holy place of St Michael by the mouth of the
River Cowin'. The rampant ivy serves to romanticise their
bizarre legend (see pp81-2)*

DAVID & CHARLES

ACKNOWLEDGEMENTS

Among the many people who have contributed to this book, the illustrator Clare Wake and the photographer John Cleare must come first. Then I must thank my friends and colleagues, hosts and hostesses: Dorothy Bosomworth, Marian Campbell, Jonathan and Jo Fryer, Sarah Harding, Paul Hewitt, Geoffrey and Enid Lake, Mark and Stella Mason, Nigel Ramsey, Nigel Terry, Ray Wallis and Timothy Wilson. Others have helped in their professional capacities: Stephen Clews of the Corinium Museum, P.W. Davies of the National Library of Wales, Catherine Johns of the British Museum, Brother Michael of the Carmelite Fathers at Aylesford, Paul Robinson of Devizes Museum, and the staff of the Iona Community, the British Library, the London Library, the archaeological section at the Royal Commission on the Historical Monuments of England, and North London Cameras Ltd.

I am most grateful to C & J Clark Ltd of Street, the shoe manufacturers, who have partly sponsored the research, and to publishers for permission to quote from their books: Routledge (*Roman Bath Discovered* by Barry Cunliffe) and Oxford University Press (*The Matter of Wales* by Jan Morris). Thanks also to Vivienne Wells, for helpful advice.

Last but not least, I salute the anonymous vicars, vergers, custodians, farmers, shepherds, locals out walking the dog and sages in the pub, for this book includes many of their pearls.

British Library Cataloguing in Publication Data
Sugden, Keith
  Walking the pilgrim ways.
  1. Great Britain
  1. Title II. Cleare, John III. Wake, Clare
  248.4630941

  ISBN 0-7153-9408-8

Typeset by ABM Typographics Ltd, Hull
and printed in Hong Kong
by Wing King Tong Co. Ltd
for David & Charles plc
Brunel House Newton Abbot Devon

CONTENTS

INTRODUCTION

Walking is a pleasure in itself, but for me the real excitement lies in viewing the landscape: every twist in the footpath has a hidden meaning and every embankment tells a story.

I have long been fascinated by the idea of pilgrimage and ancient highways, following some inner force to travel to Jerusalem, Rome and all the forgotten stations on the way. At first it surprised me to see how readily other pilgrim wayfarers responded to the combination of physical hardship along the road and the secret joy of a spiritual journey. Then, having plucked the chord, I realised that my feet would never stop itching until I had explored the old pilgrim ways of Britain and written down the story for posterity.

The routes described in this book have been selected carefully to give as much variety and as pleasant a walking environment as possible. First, the landscape ranges from mountainous terrain in the Western Isles to the flat land of the Fens, with plenty of interludes on chalk ridges, spectacular coastal paths and across rolling farmland. Secondly, the shrines are spread all over Britain, from Iona in the North, to Canterbury in the East and St Michael's Mount in the South West; while these three shrines are all famous, other routes take the reader to some of the least visited but most remarkable places on our island, like St David's on the Celtic tip of South Wales. The third variety comes in period, for the heyday of the pilgrimage routes described ranges from the first century BC (Glastonbury) to the present day (Walsingham). Lastly, the themes of the journeys vary. Superficially there is the distinction between the first two pagan journeys and the last eight Christian pilgrimages. But within this structure is displayed the development of Christianity itself, because four of the shrines are chosen to illustrate the time of the early missionaries, their struggles with heathen natives, the Viking marauders and the Roman church. The theme of two shrines is holy wells, and this pagan water lore occurs at other places, too. Gothic architecture, Scottish burial customs, Protestant suppression, Catholic resistance and the revival of pilgrimage in our own time populate other routes – there is, in fact, a theme to suit everyone's taste.

Each of the maps used in this book displays the theme of the pilgrimage in its decorative style and in the objects that it illustrates in the margins. Do not be deceived, however, by the illustrator's skill in making them works of art, for each map has been drawn meticulously to scale, so that every twist and turn of the recommended path is shown in its correct relation to the surrounding features. The intention is that intending walkers will select the route which interests them most, and then transfer the details from our maps to the larger scale Ordnance Survey maps (the 1: 50,000 Landranger series is sufficient in all cases) for use in the field. Careful comparison of our maps with the OS will reveal exactly which marked footpath, bridleway, track or country lane is the intended route. *Please note that the scale of our maps varies according to the length of the route.*

Practical information for each pilgrimage is condensed into a 'facts box'. You will see that these boxes are not entirely consistent – the routes' individual character means that the necessary information varies. For example, in only two cases do I give details suggesting escape routes to telephone boxes because exploration revealed that in other circumstances a walker in an emergency is likely to find a house with a telephone. Again, Mull is not a great place to go pub crawling as there is little opportunity and the people disapprove of strong drink, so the route to Iona has no list of pubs.

This lovely Cornish church in its graveyard full of exotic trees is called St Perran in Sabulo. The name recalls its predecessor's site among the rolling sand dunes close to St Piran's Oratory (see pp50-1)

I have explored personally every footpath, mountain pass and ford. Readers should expect to get their feet wet occasionally and, if they wear shorts, to get their legs stung by nettles and scratched by thorns. I have not personally supped ale in every pub listed under practical information, nor slept in every guest-house. This information comes from personal observation and recommendation, aided by the annual advice of the *Good Pub Guide* (Consumers'Association) and *Staying off the Beaten Track* (by Elizabeth Gundrey). Much of the exploration was made with a tent, but a useful tip is to approach the local tourist offices before you set off and ask them to send you a list of houses in the local area which offer bed and breakfast accommodation.

This is not just a book for walkers. Using our maps, cyclists will be able, in nearly all cases, to follow the historic routes quite closely by keeping to bridleways and lanes along, or close to, the marked path. Bartholomew's maps at a scale of 1: 100,000 would be more appropriate in this case. The routes to Iona, Lindisfarne, York, Walsingham, St David's, Bath and Canterbury are particularly suitable for bicycles.

Motorists who are more interested in the history and landscape than in strenuous travelling will also find that these pilgrimages make fascinating tours, and most of the sites described can be reached by lanes one way or another.

Last, but not least, the book has been written for the armchair traveller and we hope that our drawings and photographs will evoke the spirit of each pilgrimage during the long winter evenings. The pilgrimages are arranged in chronological order of their themes, which explains why the pagan routes come first. This choice allows the story to unfold more easily than if they were placed in geographical order.

The tradition of pilgrimage in Britain stretches well back to the Bronze Age nearly four thousand years ago when the famous temples at Stonehenge and Avebury on Salisbury Plain were the centres of the astounding Wessex civilisation. However, there is little evidence to show who visited these temples and why, so we begin in Chapters 1 and 2 on firmer ground with a later group of immigrants,

the Celts, who arrived, ultimately from the area now known as Austria, only a few hundred years before Christ. The following four routes cover the exciting days of the early Church when intrepid missionaries converted the Britons to Christianity. All four shrines are on the coast, neatly recalling that those Celtic saints travelled by sea. The journeys to Canterbury and York are set in the high Middle Ages when pilgrimage reached its greatest popularity. The shrine at Holywell reflects the Reformation and the strength of the Catholic resistance to it. The time sequence and the book end with the great twentieth-century revival of pilgrimage to Our Lady of Walsingham.

Throughout the book historic buildings and sites are identified by a six-figure map reference to help you to find them in the field – it is not an encouragement to go treasure-hunting. Most of the archaeological sites are scheduled and it is a criminal offence to interfere with them. In those few cases where the remains do not enjoy statutory protection, the landowner can sue for trespass. If you see any suspicious characters with metal detectors around a site they are robbing you of your heritage; please record any details such as car number-plates and report them both to the police and to the relevant Royal Commission on Historical Monuments – there are separate branches for England, Scotland and Wales.

· PILGRIMAGE THROUGH THE AGES

Celtic Mystery

Avebury and Stonehenge, the two most important prehistoric temples in Britain, are sited in close proximity, being located at the centre of the map as far as ancient tracks are concerned. Many ridgeways converge on Salisbury Plain, having followed the dry ridges which were free of natural dense woodland from Cornwall, the south coast, Kent, East Anglia, the Midlands, the North and Wales. This is why neolithic man chose Salisbury Plain to construct the massive henge at Avebury and the later temple at Stonehenge. We can confidently say that these temples were the first places of pilgrimage in the British Isles; but unfortunately, we know little about why men visited them and what rituals were conducted in or around them, especially in the case of Avebury.

Much is known about the religion of the Celts, on the other hand, who invaded Britain in about 500BC. Certainly the evil spirits which inhabited their Otherworld were an ever-present and dangerous force requiring propitiation. But the Celts also worshipped an enormous number of deities, who were often so local that they are known at one shrine only. Frequently the god or goddess lived in a spring – an obvious source of nature's bounty – which explains why Celtic temples are often situated near wells and streams and why there are so many holy wells today, some for healing and others for cursing.

The Druids, who were a high caste among the Celts, were in part priests, philosophers, judges and teachers, and they were one of the few groups who were able to move freely between the territories of the warlike tribes. They wrote down nothing of their beliefs deliberately and only the propaganda of their enemies attests to their practice of human sacrifice.

The Christians Adapt the Pagan Ways

At a few places in Britain tradition or modern research claims that Christianity never died out in the Dark Ages: Glastonbury in Somerset and Deerhurst in Gloucestershire are among this select group. Evangelists generally found that it was prudent to adapt the pagan beliefs to the new religion, rather than simply to destroy them, taking on board the old myths and sacred sites. A famous letter from Pope Gregory the Great to St Augustine instructs the sixth-century missionary to build his churches on ancient places of worship. So the early Christian pilgrimages described here are imbued with the old beliefs and are all the richer for it.

The Celtic Church was a bastion of learning and artistic endeavour in a barbarous Europe and its contacts were international. The early monks moved at will between western Britain – Dumnonia (the Cornish peninsula), Wales and Dalriada (the west of Scotland) – Ireland and Brittany, exploiting their common language. In those times any learned man with charisma, initiative and the ability to lead others could become a saint, for any-

one who successfully founded a new church was likely to be canonised after a respectable interval by their congregation – for example, St Carantoc in Cornwall – such was the independence of each community under the Celtic rule. Energetic monks like Patrick, Columba, David or Piran, to take only one saint from each country, were held in such esteem by their brethren and followers that their churches soon became shrines to their memory and pilgrims braved every hardship to gain wisdom, guidance, comfort or healing from their physical remains.

Brendan's Voyage

A Celtic monk called Brendan (c486-575) and several companions made a famous voyage by coracle from Britain, probably reaching Iceland, Greenland or North America, which appears in written form about three centuries after his death. The *Voyage of St Brendan* enjoyed great popularity in the later Middle Ages – there are no less than 116 surviving manuscripts of the Latin version. It is a curious allegory of discovery, sometimes describing nature in minute detail – for example, the life of seals – and at other times waxing mystical, as in the episode where Brendan discovers on a huge iceberg a chalice and paten apparently made of ice. But the significance of the allegory lies in the deliberate endurance of hardship in order to discover the truth, whether it was geographical or spiritual.

St Augustine and his followers began their mission to England by converting the Saxon royal families to Christianity; from that point the faith of each king led to the replacement of pagan beliefs by Christian ones. Some monarchs became so devout that saving their own souls took precedence over ruling the kingdom. Such was King Ina of Wessex, who gave his throne to a kinsman and made the 'permanent pilgrimage' to Rome, founding there the English hospice in 727 (which still exists close to the Vatican). Many wealthy Englishmen of the day followed his example, trusting that, by dying at Rome close to the bearer of the keys of heaven (St Peter), they would stand the best possible chance of entering heaven on the Day of Judgement.

In those early Christian days only the wealthy could afford the ultimate pilgrimage to Rome;

St Brendan's voyage in about AD530. The coracle is based on the reconstruction used by Tim Severin in his 1977 re-enactment

common Englishmen had to rest content with visiting a local shrine in their own county. Even then the choice of shrines must have been wide, with the memory of the foundation of their churches still fresh in the minds of the people, and the relics of hundreds of founders ('saints') close at hand. By the time pilgrimage reached its heyday in the fourteenth century, it was an extremely popular occupation: the recorded number of pilgrims who travelled to Canterbury for many years exceeded two hundred thousand, out of a total population in England estimated at nearly four million on the outbreak of the Black Death in 1348. The number of famous shrines grew and grew as monks and prelates vied to attract more pilgrims: each individual church was supposed to have a relic of some

kind. Many judged the fame of towns, not on the size of the population or the quality of their products, but on the number and reputation of their relics. Some shrines had connections with numerous saints – there were thirteen at Glastonbury, for example, excluding King Arthur – while others possessed more relics than the clergy knew what to do with – for example, over four hundred were itemised at Canterbury.

Pilgrims in the High Middle Ages

The first stage of the pilgrim's journey was the ceremony to mark his leaving his home parish. After Mass and special prayers, the priest would consecrate the pilgrim's *scrip* (a wallet similar to a modern fishing bag) and *bourdon* (his tall staff), sprinkling each with holy water. Then the pilgrim's friends and relations would lead him out of the village with the cross borne high before them and give him their blessing at the parish boundary. The

INTRODUCTION

pilgrim was also supposed to carry a letter from his priest or his temporal lord to act as a recommendation of his genuine status to the pious and the charitable whom he would meet along the way.

The pilgrim would have considered it both an honour and a penance to wear his costume, which served to identify him and to help him in begging for alms on his pilgrimage. He wore a long and coarse woollen robe, which was brown or russet in colour and big enough to wrap himself up in for sleeping. A cross decorated the sleeve. His large round hat had a broad brim, usually turned up at the front to display his pilgrim badges – the symbolic shell and leaden images from the shrines he had already visited. Slung on lanyards around his neck he carried a scrip, a large knife, a flask for water and a rosary. The scrip was for spare pairs of hosen, two days' food and essential ointment for his feet. He also carried a long stout staff, which was used for vaulting over streams, climbing hills

and as defence against outlaws. Sometimes the staff was tipped with a hollow metal ball, the jangling 'Canterbury bell'.

The pilgrim who had a home to return to, was distinct from the palmer, who had none. The palmer was a professional pilgrim who lived entirely on alms and journeyed perpetually from shrine to shrine. Men knew him by the palm, or branch, brought back from the Holy Land. The palmer's way of life was a convenient cover for a variety of escaped villeins (feudal tenants) and criminals, or those who found a settled existence or their fellow men unbearable. In modern terms, they were tramps who were adept at taking advantage of those common souls who shunned them.

Wearing the outfit: a pilgrim on a medieval road. Note the shell in his hat, the bourdon *or staff, the wallet, drinking bottle, rough woollen clothing and unshorn hair, all signs of the true pilgrim*

If a man was too sick, too busy, or too lazy to go on a pilgrimage himself, it was common practice for him to employ a proxy to make the journey on his behalf, and the Church prudently recognised this as being just as effective as making the journey himself. More commonly, a pilgrimage would take place by proxy after a would-be pilgrim had died to gain some favour for his soul on the Day of Judgement: funds would be specified by will for the purpose.

Motives and Benefits

Usually people went on a pilgrimage for religious reasons, but sometimes they had a secular motive. The pilgrim's main intention was to pray at a shrine, where he or she would appeal directly to the saint concerned for success in a venture, whether in business, love or war, or for a cure to an illness or disability. Vows made at home, in a church or even in the heat of battle, often obliged the believer to make a long journey to a shrine as a thanksgiving for safe deliverance. It was also customary for a priest to impose a particular pilgrimage on a repentant soul in the confessional as a suitable penance for sins committed.

Other motives determined a person's intention to take up the scrip and staff, especially when pilgrimage became very popular. People would go on a pilgrimage to make a public affirmation of their faith, or in the hope that they would reap a reward. The curious and the adventurous would go to add interest to their lives, and would enjoy the display at a shrine, which was often the most lavish artistry that they would ever see in their lives.

The pilgrim's costume provided anonymity for a criminal on the run or a villein escaping from the bondage of his lord of the manor, as well as being an acceptable disguise for the beggar. The more talented vagrant might make a living from entertaining his fellow pilgrims, or, if he had the effrontery, a considerable profit from selling indulgences. Such was the rich tapestry of pilgrim life.

By the late fourteenth century (Chaucer wrote *The Canterbury Tales* in the 1390s) pilgrims were a motley group, made up mainly of men, with characters as varied as their occupations and rank in society. Kings and nobles would sometimes endow shrines and hospices with large sums of money, and the gifts of pilgrims helped to build and rebuild many cathedrals and abbeys – and, incidentally, served to line the pockets of many an outlaw. The poorest class of freemen had to rely on alms to enable them to make a pilgrimage and return home. The *demi-monde* of criminals and tramps – a band of surly troublemakers – were tolerated because they assumed the pilgrim's guise.

Stations on the Road

Crosses were once a common sight along the roadside. Old maps and archaeological records indicate where some of them once stood, and although the crosses themselves have totally disappeared, stone bases can still be found on roadside verges. Crosses often occupied sites where they could be seen from a great distance – for example the 'Legs Cross' beside the B6275 to Hexham in Northumberland stands silhouetted against the sky at the top of a ridge. Otherwise they are found at old crossroads, such as Cockley Cley wayside cross which is marked on the Green Way (TF 792027) to Walsingham by the Victorian Ordnance Survey. Wayside crosses gradually disappeared, either because they were made of wood, or because they were used to repair the nearby road or walling. Crosses served as waymarks to reassure travellers that they were on the right road and as roadside shrines where travellers could offer prayers for a safe journey or in thanksgiving for thwarting a robber. This custom is still very popular in Greece, where isolated roadside shrines contain devotional items.

Much grander pilgrim crosses were built on roads that led to important shrines. As they were more monumental than ordinary wayside crosses some have survived – for example, two may be found on village greens in Norfolk, one at Binham on the road to Walsingham from the east and the other at Hockwold cum Wilton on the road to Walsingham from the south.

Chapels were built along the pilgrim routes especially for the devotion of passing travellers. St Martha's and St Catherine's on the Pilgrims' Way near Guildford are two well-known pilgrim chapels, one in ruins and the other much restored. The best preserved pilgrim chapel in England is undoubtedly the Red Mount Chapel at King's Lynn, Norfolk, a lovely octagonal tower of brickwork on an artificial knoll. It stands near the crossing of the River Ouse where Walsingham-bound pilgrims lost their pilgrim badges in the mud of the Purfleet; these are now on display in King's Lynn Museum.

Pilgrim Hospices

A pilgrimage was usually made during the summer months, so it is probable that pilgrims often slept under a hedge or in a barn. The specialised accom-modation which survives in England from the hey-day of pilgrimage-making varies from hospices run by monks or by a dedicated charity, to monasteries whose rules obliged the brethren to offer hospi-tality to *any* traveller, to common inns.

The Hospital of Newark at Maidstone was a fine example of a hospice supported by a charity. Archbishop Boniface built it in 1261 to receive pil-grims on their way to Canterbury, although it is several miles from the Pilgrims' Way. Only its Early English chapel survives, which is used as the chancel of St Peter's Church. At nearby Aylesford, where the old road actually crossed the Medway, a unique pilgrims' hall survives, built as a private charity by Baron de Grey as early as 1170 (see p113). In this hall they would have slept as well as eaten.

Large halls were needed to accommodate pil-grims at the popular shrines. The Stranger's Hall at the shrine of St Swithun in Winchester was such a guest-house, run by the Benedictine monks within their precinct; it survives today as part of the Deanery.

Canterbury had many hospices, such as the Hospital of St Thomas the Martyr, now known as the King's Bridge Hospital, and founded, according to its charter, by the 'glorious St Thomas the Martyr to receive poor wayfaring men'. The Norman crypt and later refectory and chapel can still be seen. Other pilgrims lodged in the great priory of Christ Church (the cathedral), where a fifteenth-century extension known as Chillenden's Guest Chamber survives as part of the Bishop of Dover's

house. Smaller numbers of pilgrims dispersed to the Hospital of St John in Northgate, the great Augustinian abbey, or to guest-houses run by the mendicant friars.

The duty of the Knights Templar and the Knights Hospitaller was to protect and succour pil-grims on their way to the Holy Land. However, neither group carried out this duty systematically along the pilgrimage routes in Britain; they acquired property more by chance, for example when knights surrendered their estates to the orders, which was a requirement on joining. So only occasionally did the Knights run hospices, as at Templeton (Templars' Town) in south Pem-brokeshire, on one of the roads to St David's.

Some inns, such as the George and Pilgrims at Glastonbury in Somerset, the White Horse at Shere in Surrey (on the Pilgrims' Way to Canter-bury), and the Bell at Tewkesbury in Gloucester-shire (on the road to the Holy Blood at Hayles Abbey), were built especially for the pilgrim traffic. All of these inns, incidentally, survive to the present day. Unfortunately, the most famous pilgrim inn of all, 'The Chequers of the Hope, which every man doth know', where Chaucer's pilgrims stayed when they reached Canterbury, burnt down a century ago – only its cellars survive, along with the memory of its 'dormitory of the hundred beds'.

The Abuse of Indulgences

The profligate sale of indulgences is probably the most notorious of all the papal abuses cited by the Protestant reformers of Luther's day. An in-dulgence was a document issued by the Pope that absolved the sinner from temporal punishment. Spaces were left for the applicant's name, the period of its validity and other details. An in-dulgence was a document issued by the pope that nation, but it did excuse him from doing penance for his misdeeds.

Indulgences were attached automatically to certain pilgrimages. Pilgrims who went to the Holy Land received the best indulgences – a plenary in-dulgence that lasted 'seven years and seven lents' at every holy place – and they returned to England laden with so many as to constitute a licence to sin for the rest of their lives. Pilgrims who could not

travel to Jerusalem would journey to Rome, to receive the second-best indulgences. There pilgrims would visit the four patriarchal churches or the seven pilgrimage churches, as well as other shrines.

The shrines at Santiago (Sant Iago = St James) de Compostella in north-west Spain and at Canterbury were equally ranked after Rome for the value of their relics. Nowadays, St Thomas Becket's shrine in Canterbury is considered of greater importance as the authenticity of St James' relics has been seriously questioned. Papal bulls allowed comparisons to be made between some medieval shrines; thus, two pilgrimages made to St David's Cathedral in Wales were considered equal to one pilgrimage to Rome.

Monks' Tricks

The most famous deception by monks was the Boxley Rood of Grace, an ingenious automaton with an astonishing range of facial expressions which was controlled by the custodian through a system of wires in response to the value of the pilgrim's monetary offering. The image could frown, wag its head, foam at the mouth, weep and raise its hands in blessing. The secret of the deception was well kept. Only at the dissolution of the monasteries did Henry VIII's commissioners reveal the truth.

The duplication of relics reached farcical proportions: there were numerous girdles that supposedly belonged to the Virgin Mary and at least ten skulls of John the Baptist. When a sixteenth-century pilgrim at a French monastery was shown a John the Baptist head he remarked that he had seen the skull of the same saint only the day before at another monastery. 'Maybe,' the monk replied, 'that was the skull of John the Baptist when a young man, whereas this in our possession is his skull after he was fully advanced in years and wisdom.'

The wide expanses of the Wiltshire Downs seen from the path to Glastonbury. The viewpoint is close to the Iron Age fort at Hanging Langford Camp, looking north-northeast across the Wylye valley towards the Harrow Way, the prehistoric ridgeway from Dover to Salisbury Plain and the Westcountry

A monk stealing a relic in the twelfth century

In England the bones of St Dunstan became the subject of a long and bitter dispute between the monks of Glastonbury and Canterbury, with both churches claiming possession of the true relics. The Glastonbury monks asserted that they had rescued the saint's remains from the smouldering ruins of Canterbury Cathedral, and they successfully maintained the pretence until 1508.

As relics became more and more of a cult the riches they could generate stimulated their theft – for example, in 1020 a pilgrim stole the Venerable Bede's relics and took them to Durham, where they still rest in the cathedral's Galilee Chapel. Later, elaborate precautions were taken to protect relics against theft: shrines were usually designed with holes that were large enough for pilgrims to see the reliquary inside but too small for it to be removed.

Monks kept watch from lofts above the shrines and visitors often had to leave the sanctuary through a tiny door where they might be stopped and searched.

Arriving at the Shrine

For a charming description of the devout and genuine pilgrim, we can do no better than to turn to the pen of J. J. Jusserand:

Arrived at the end of their journey, all prayed; prayed with fervour in the humblest posture. The soul was filled with religous emotion when from the end of the majestic alley formed by the coloured twilight of the nave, the heart divined, rather than the eye saw, the mysterious object of veneration for which such a distance had been traversed at the cost of such fatigue. Though the practical man galloped up to bargain with the saint for the favour of God, though the emissary sent to make offering in the name of his master might keep a dry and clear eye, tears coursed down the cheeks of the poor and simple in heart. He tasted fully of the pious emotion he had come to seek, the peace of heaven descended into his bosom, and he went away consoled. Such was the happy lot of simple, devout souls.

The Reformation and Dissolution

The decline in the popularity of pilgrimages began before the sixteenth century. Even before Henry VIII established the Anglican Church in 1534, miraculous relics had come to be regarded with scepticism and even genuine relics had lost their power to draw the faithful. Thomas Cromwell and his commissioners destroyed the medieval shrines with remarkable alacrity. For example, in March 1538 Henry VIII lit a candle before the image of Our Lady of Walsingham, but only a few months later his men seized the candle and cast it, together with relics and images that had been stripped from churches all over the country, onto a huge pyre in Chelsea. The shrines that had been venerated for centuries were stripped of their treasures, while the walls that had been worn smooth by the touch of countless pilgrims' hands were left to collapse.

Survival and Revival

Holywell in North Wales is a shrine that was never abandoned by the adherents of the old faith. During the Middle Ages this ancient pagan well became one of the most popular Christian places of pilgrimage. During the Reformation, for reasons which remain obscure, it also became a focus of activity by Catholic recusants. Pilgrims never stopped coming to the shrine, despite the best efforts of the Anglican bishop and the civil power. Today this shrine is still visited by thousands of pilgrims every year – not too many people, though, to destroy the peace of this most ornamental of Gothic chapels, but enough to keep the candles burning constantly.

During the twentieth century Anglicans and Catholics have revived the royal pilgrimage to Walsingham (see Chaper 10). There are separate Anglican and Catholic shrines, but neither is on the original sacred site. Canterbury, too, has benefited from this modern enthusiasm for an old custom. More genuine pilgrims now arrive at the shrine of St Thomas Becket than at any time since 1500.

In the far west of Ireland three shrines maintain a strong hold on their devotees. Nowhere else in the British Isles is pilgrimage taken more seriously than at Lough Derg in County Donegal, where pilgrims assemble on St Patrick's Island on the saint's day for an extremely rigorous three-day penance to commemorate his fast. During that period no boatman is available to row anyone other than true pilgrims across to the island.

Croagh Patrick is a mountain of rock and scree on the Atlantic coast of County Mayo where St Patrick meditated for forty days and prayed that Ireland should remain forever Christian. On the last Sunday in July – 'Reek Sunday' as it is known – some sixty thousand Roman Catholics commemorate St Patrick's devotion. It is, in the words of Paul Barker (*The Independent*, 12 August 1989),

> an extraordinary, almost medieval sight. Above you, the line stretches along the brow of Ireland's Holy Mountain till it disappears in the thickening cloud. Below you, hundreds more are on their way up or down. The young are in everything from multi-coloured anoraks and trainers to satin jackets and high heels; the old in tweed jackets and brown boots, like characters from *The Irish RM*.

At Knock, also in County Mayo, pilgrims visit the site of a vision that was witnessed by the entire village one night in 1879. For several hours St Joseph, the Blessed Virgin Mary and the Agnus Dei appeared over the gable of the modest church. Today's Pope Paul was persuaded by the villagers of Knock to bless the site on its centenary in 1979 when they built a runway that was long enough for his airliner to land on. On that occasion no less than one million Irish men and women – one-third of the republic's population – converged on Knock. Such is the continuing power of miracles and holy places.

1

AWAY TO AVALON

A Journey to the Celtic Paradise

his chapter follows the route of a first-century pilgrimage to the entrance to the Celts' mythical land of the dead, known as Avalon. For centuries this paradise has been identified as a small but magical hill rising out of the Somerset Levels – Glastonbury Tor. Some pagan magic seems to cling there, so that to even the least spiritual person it has a peculiar attraction. Tradition asserts that the very first Christian missionaries to Britain visited Glastonbury while Jesus was still on earth, while we know that their successors built an early hermitage in the tor.

Whether the identification of Avalon with Glastonbury is correct and whether the modern mystics who flourish in the town are all mistaken in their beliefs or are poseurs, readers must decide for themselves. But in this book we could not ignore perhaps the holiest sanctuary in Britain just because mystery and controversy surround the tor.

In Celtic times horsemen would have approached Avalon from the east because of the lakes and swamps which surrounded the island. A prehistoric causeway crossed the marshes and it is still in use as the modern A361. It penetrates an important earthwork called Ponter's Ball whose significance will become clear later.

A suitable starting place for our journey is the Iron Age hillfort at Old Sarum, on a prominent hilltop just to the north of Salisbury. Situated to the east of Glastonbury, it was an important town during Celtic times; it also possesses a ridgeway leading westwards which eventually connects with the prehistoric causeway across to Avalon.

The geographical importance of Old Sarum for prehistoric communications becomes clear from a glance at the map. This is the place where the five rivers meet like the fingers of a human hand: the Bourne, the Avon, the Wylye, the Nadder and the Ebble. This means that it is also the place where six ridgeways meet, funnelling travellers from all of Wessex into the broad Avon Valley. This slow-flowing river reaches the splendid anchorage at Christchurch Harbour, which is protected from the open sea by Hengistbury Head. It is easy to see that the carriage of so much trade from all of Wessex and points beyond to the south coast and the Continent gave Old Sarum a considerable strategic and commercial role. Finds of Mediterranean burial gifts in Bronze Age tumuli confirm the importance of Old Sarum from an early period.

· OLD SARUM ·

The Iron Age hillfort at Old Sarum strengthens a hill at the western end of a promontory of the downlands. The huge circular rampart overlooks a wide area of countryside, but especially the traffic up the Avon Valley into central Wessex. A likely date for the hillfort's construction is about 500BC. Old Sarum's fortifications always remained simple – a single bank and ditch with only one entrance, which was protected by a straightforward 'hornwork'. The owners, a warlike tribe called the Durotriges, occupied Old Sarum as a small town and refuge for surrounding settlements. The Durotriges' main enemies on this frontier would have been the Atrebates to the east.

The earthworks show no evidence of hasty fortification in the face of the Roman advance, so this hillfort may have been surrendered in favour of stronger positions. The Romans pacified the Durotriges in AD44, but then let the territory become a backwater, in sharp contrast to the heavily Romanised Cotswolds. Numerous excavations have revealed only scant traces of Roman occupa-

tion within the hillfort. It seems that the station they established to control the important junction of five of their roads should be sought at Stratford sub Castle on the left bank of the Avon. They called the place Sorviodunum, which means 'the fort by the slow-moving river'.

Life in the Iron Age

To bring life to these scenes from the first century we must take a brief look at how the Iron Age farmers lived.

Fields were roughly square and extended from $\frac{1}{3}$ to $1\frac{1}{2}$ acres (0.1-0.6ha); on unploughed downland their banks are easily seen. Wheat and barley were the staple crops. Milk was stored by making cheese. Peas, beans and lentils were the basic vegetables. The domestication of bees was already long established, so mead was fermented as well as beer.

Each autumn all the non-breeding livestock was slaughtered because of the shortage of winter feed. This meat would have been salted or smoked rather than air-dried because of the wet climate.

Domestic crafts were weaving, thatching, hurdling, netting, basketry, lathe-turned ornaments and implements, pottery and boat-building, especially skin-covered coracles. Metal-working was not a domestic but a specialist trade, and the goldsmith enjoyed a high status. Britons were famous on the Continent for their hunting dogs, and their other known exports are corn, cattle, tin, gold, hides and slaves.

Later Development of the Hillfort

Following the Saxon conquest of Wessex, Old Sarum lay derelict for three centuries until King Alfred's subjects refortified it against Danish, and later against Viking, attacks. The Normans transferred the Saxon bishop's seat from Sherborne, Dorset, to Old Sarum. Old Sarum cathedral was soon destroyed by fire; a second Norman cathedral, whose foundations we now see here, was built and extended westwards. The impressive earthwork in the middle of the hillfort is the inner bailey of the Norman castle. The whole hilltop became a dramatic military town, rather like Durham, for about two centuries. With the bishop's decision in the thirteeenth century to establish the splendid new city of Salisbury in the plain to the south, Old Sarum was gradually abandoned.

· AWAY TO AVALON: THE ROUTE ·

On considering the viable Iron Age routes from Old Sarum to Glastonbury three possibilities occur. One way is to travel along the important prehistoric trackway which broadly follows the line of the modern A303. This would be a long way round but would pass the large hillforts of Yarnbury Castle, White Sheet Hill and South Cadbury. The approach to Glastonbury, however, would be across the marshes from the south and there is no evidence that this route was possible in prehistoric times.

A more direct line would be a riverside route along the banks of the Wylye, which may have been the northern boundary of the warlike Durotriges, as far as Warminster and perhaps beyond. This would run underneath the hillforts of Grovely Castle, Bilbury Rings, Scratchbury Hill and Battlebury Camp. But in this case the going might have been tough, for the lower ground was probably such thick forest that a track would have been impossible.

The most likely choice is the direct ridgeway which is marked out as an early Wessex track by R. Hippisley Cox in his book *The Green Roads of England*. The route was improved soon after the Roman conquest of Britain, probably in order to pacify the Durotriges and to exploit the extensive mines on the Mendip Hills. (The evidence for the early date lies in finds of pigs – that is, ingots – of Roman lead on the same road but east of Old Sarum.) This is altogether an excellent Iron Age road, for it is direct, as well as high and dry. Its whole line as far as Creech Hill (within sight of the Isle of Avalon) was thickly settled in the period, as is shown by the numerous remains of stock enclosures and settlements still visible today. As for the actual form of Iron Age roads, little evidence exists, but heavy carts that have been found in Iron Age burials indicate the existence of at least some proper roads which were wider than simple mule-tracks. In special conditions elaborate work was

ROBIN HOOD'S BOWER

LONGBRIDGE
DEVERILL

LONGBARROW

BRIXTON
DEVERILL

COLD KITCHEN HILL

LONG BARROW

KINGSTON
DEVERILL

MONKTON
DEVERILL

PERTWOOD DOWN
CEMETERY

ROMAN RD

ROMAN RD

ROMAN RD

GREAT RIDGE

STOCKTON EARTHWORKS

SCRUBBEDOAK

ROMAN ROAD

CRATT HILL

ANCIENT CROSSROADS

BOWL BARROW

KEYSLEY
DOWN

A303

TUMULUS

CHARNAGE DOWN

HILL FORT

TEMPLE

FARM SETTLEMENT

STOCK ENCLOSURE

FIELD SYSTEM

CW

AWAY TO AV
OLD SARVM TO O

GLASTONBURY

ABBEY
CHALICE WELL

GLASTONBURY TOR

WEST
PENNARD

PYLLE

A361

ANCIENT CAUSEWAY

PENNARD HILL

PONTER'S BALL

EAST
PENNARD

FOSSE WAY

WEST BRADLEY

WRAXALL

DITCHEAT

ARTHUR'S BRIDGE

SM

YARNBURY
CASTLE

WYLE

● STEEPLE LANGFORD

⌖ STAPLEFORD

RIVER WYLYE

BILBURY RINGS

EAST CASTLE

GROVELY CASTLE

CHURCH END RING

HANGING LANGFORD
CAMP

EBSBURY
SETTLEMENT

GREAT ⌖
WISHFORD

ROMAN ROAD

SOUTH NEWTON

LITTLE DURNFORD

EARTHWORK

OLD SARVM

CHILHAMPTON

AVON
BRIDGE

BARFORD DOWN

RIVER AVON

GROVELY HILL

BARFORD
ST MARTIN

WILTON

RIVER NADDER

RIVER BOURNE

SALISBURY

ALON

LITTLE WOODBURY

ASTONBVRY

ON
DON

NORTH BREWHAM

CH HILL

SOUTH BREWHAM

JACK'S CASTLE
TUMULUS

ST PETER'S
PUMP

WHITE SHEET DOWNS
NEOLITHIC
CAMP

MEDIEVAL
BOUNDARY CROSS

ALFRED'S
TOWER

PARK HILL
CAMP

STOURTON

WHITESHEET HILL

CASTLE WOOD
CAMP

KILOMETRES
MILES

possible: the Iron Age continuation of the neolithic trackway tradition across the Somerset Levels shows this.

Crossing the Rivers

Our path crosses only two proper rivers in the whole of its 46½ mile (75km) length, and both of these are in the first 3 miles (5km). Almost directly underneath the western ramparts of Old Sarum is the crossing of the River Avon that was probably used in Roman times, if not before. There is still a crossing there (SU 128330) called Avon Bridge.

Follow this lane and take the track left up the ridge past Hill Farm, follow the A360 briefly away from Wilton and then turn left (SU 112337) onto a ridge that is rich in Iron Age remains. The whole hilltop was a Romano-British farm, with a settlement at its eastern end (almost on the modern road) and two areas of field systems, which are still visible. The first irregular boundaries can be seen on the left of the track on flattish ground around SU 112336; then a large set of contour-following lynchets and banks covers 60 acres (24ha) on the right of the track between SU 106335 and SU 098330. Farmers belonging to the La Tène Celtic culture occupied the site from about 20BC to AD50. Construction of a reservoir and pipeline in 1933 revealed pot sherds, painted plaster and the remains of a small oven and flue.

The next obstacle is the River Wylye, one of the five rivers which come together at Old Sarum like the fingers of a human hand. It appears that the Romans may have used a ford (SU 088338) about 550yd (500m) downstream from the weir at South Newton Mill. Although there is a footbridge there today, you need to follow the busy A36 trunk road to reach it, so a preferable crossing is the bridge at Chilhampton.

Ways along Grovely Ridge

There are several ways of following the Grovely Ridge, which now stretches ahead for 17 miles (28km) all the way to the dramatic scarp at White Sheet Hill. Although it is now totally uninhabited, the early Britons occupied most of the downland, and their fields, stock enclosures and hillforts can be seen all along it. Half-way along, the A303 trunk

road forms an ancient crossroads, but elsewhere you will hardly see a soul.

The suggested route follows the Roman line roughly, but since the Wiltshire historian Sir Richard Colt Hoare traced the Mendip road nearly two centuries ago, many new plantations have obscured the low agger, which everywhere keeps to a constant width of about 18ft (5m). Like the Devil's Causeway in Northumberland (see Chapter 6), the indication of the course on the Ordnance Survey map should not be taken as evidence of an obvious bank on the ground, for the cartographers have simply kept up Hoare's line from edition to edition. Here on the Mendip road plantations are the culprit, whereas ploughing has obscured the Devil's Causeway.

A good alternative for cyclists is the rough trackway which follows the south side of the ridge all the way to Chicklade Bottom on the A303. Although this route does not pass as close to all the interesting Iron Age sites, it does enjoy more unobstructed views. This old lane has itself many of the characteristics of an ancient ridgeway, always keeping below the crest on the sunnier, and therefore drier, side. It begins at the prominent triple fork in the woods at SU 084324.

Celtic Farmsteads through Grovely Wood

The ridge, which stretches ahead for about 25 miles (40km) to Lamyatt, contains some of the most extensive remains of Iron Age agriculture in the whole of Britain. Between 100BC and AD500 the Durotriges developed and occupied the system of field boundaries and stock enclosures for over-wintering cattle. The survival of so much evidence of British settlement up on the ridge is due to the preference of the Saxon invaders for clearing and ploughing new land down in the valleys.

The first example of occupation by Iron Age farmers is a large Durotrigian native settlement known as Hamshill Ditches which lies on the south side of the path. The remains of the settlement itself are well preserved in the woodland, and among the hut foundations is a suspected temple platform (SU 065330). The system of roughly rectangular fields extends for 2 miles (3km) along the hillside between the edge of the wood and the lane along

the contour below. A network of trackways connects them together, and there is an outlier of the same field system out to the west at Swindley Copse (SU 017340).

Ebsbury settlement has a similar field system on the other side of the Grovely Ridge and our path. It stretches for over 1 mile (2km) along the contours from Ebsbury Hill to beyond Grovely Castle (SU 048358). This small hillfort encloses 13 acres (5ha) inside a single rampart on a promontory, but it lost its purpose with the Roman conquest and the field boundaries actually overlie the defences.

The next main settlement is confusingly called Hanging Langford Camp because its earthworks were once thought to be defensive. On the complex site, excavated by Salisbury Museum in 1961, is a field system on the hill connected to a 'banjo-shaped' earthwork in the valley to the north, called Church-end Ring, which is probably some kind of stock enclosure. Along a promontory to the northeast is another confusing name, East Castle, a roughly circular earthwork (SU 030361) which was probably a separate farm but which contains a

The Roman road from Winchester and Old Sarum to the Mendip lead mines crossed the River Wylye at this ford

bowl barrow. Hanging Langford did have its own defences, a circular hillfort of 17 acres (7ha) with several ramparts on rather flat ground – Bilbury Rings (SU 010363) are now rather worn down and surround a modern farm with an Iron Age straight ditch connecting them to their settlement.

Although we have passed extensive native farms, this does not indicate that Iron Age times were peaceful. Simply look at Bilbury Rings and Grovely Castle, two little hillforts which are situated less than 2½ miles (4km) apart. In this upland territory of the Durotriges in south Wiltshire and Dorset more than seventy hillforts dominate the landscape of chalk downs. Such a density of fortifications speaks volumes about the fear of neighbouring tribes in this part of Britain before the Roman conquest.

At Hanging Langford our path along the line of the Roman road finally emerges from the mixed plantations of Grovely Wood and continues as a

winding trackway across an area of open farmland. After 2½ miles (4km) we reach an ancient crossing of two ridgeways: the modern A303 actually follows a prehistoric route that links the hillforts at Yarnbury and Cadbury.

The path immediately crosses the fourth and largest of all the Durotrigian settlements on Grovely Ridge: the village known as Stockton Earthworks (ST 970362) occupies 62 acres (25ha). Among the numerous irregular ditches and mounds, hollow ways can be traced between the sites of houses, all of which are surrounded by the remains of a disused hillfort from an earlier period. Finds from the many excavations on this site may be seen in Devizes and Salisbury museums. The huge Stockton field system covers 500 acres (200ha) to the north and east of the settlement. The many individual fields and lynchets are seen most easily when a slanting sun picks out their shadows, because ploughing has reduced the sharp relief of the banks. The Durotrigians also had another 120 acres (48ha) to the west on Sherrington Down (ST 956365), but only faint traces are now visible on the ground. Stockton probably had many more fields but these have completely disappeared.

The Ridgeway to White Sheet Castle

Our path continues along the ridge as a bridleway which picks up the course of the Roman road again through Great Ridge Wood. The trees conceal four irregular enclosures which are each typically about 65yd (60m) long. Their isolated positions away from a system of fields means that they were corrals used for overwintering the precious breeding stock.

Where the bridleway emerges from Great Ridge Wood there are the scanty remains of another native field system called Cratt Hill (ST 903362). But as soon as the track crosses the A350 we are more in the land of the dead than of the living, for Pertwood Down on the right is thick with prehistoric burial mounds. They are all ploughed

The actual line of the Roman road from Old Sarum to the Mendip lead mines as it passes close to Hanging Langford Camp on Grovely Ridge. The eighteeenth century Wiltshire antiquary Sir Richard Colt Hoare surveyed its course

down to less than a third of their original height of about 3yd (3m), but they can still be recognised as shallow circular ditches 11-22yd (10-20m) in diameter. The tireless antiquary Sir Richard Colt Hoare dug one out in 1807 and found a skeleton.

Here a footpath turns south to follow the top of a scarp to Charnage Down via Keysley Farm. Just to the south-west of the farm is a much better preserved bowl barrow (ST 861351) 22yd (20m) in diameter and 2yd (2m) high. Once again Colt Hoare got here first. A detour to the south-east will reach a group of two more prominent mounds, a long barrow and a bowl barrow, at Willoughby Hedge (ST 879341).

Continuing south-west from Keysley Farm a stiff clay track turns right just before the main A303 and continues along a new ridge in our previous westerly direction. On the left of the path is the Charnage Down stock enclosure (ST 842341) and field system. The settlement bank, which is about 55yd (50m) square and overgrown with nettles, is nearby.

Excitement mounts as the track approaches by far the grandest monument along the whole ridge: White Sheet Castle Iron Age hillfort (ST 804345). Attackers could approach along two necks of the downs, but prominent cross dykes defend them both. The scarp drops away so steeply on the south and east that the Durotriges built only one rampart on those sides, but enemies who penetrated the cross dykes would have had to have faced the onslaught of sling shots from warriors on three successive ramparts on the third side. It shows at least two phases of construction and Iron Age pot sherds have been found on the surface.

The ramparts protect two well-preserved ring barrows, an unusual form with no mound, but with a circular embankment outside a ditch that encloses the burial in the middle of a flat platform. After crossing the northern cross dyke of the hillfort our path enters the White Sheet Downs neolithic causewayed enclosure, built by the first farmers in Britain in about 3000BC. The pear-shaped earthwork is about 240yd (220m) long. Test excavations by Stuart Piggott revealed some pottery of the Windmill Hill type, but not the function of these curious camps which were certainly not defensive.

The Iron Age hillfort called White Sheet Castle in Wiltshire. Three banks protect the level side, but only one is needed on the scarp sides

Beating the Bounds

The plateau that surrounds White Sheet Hill is a nature reserve and one of the best preserved areas of chalk downlands remaining in Wiltshire, which can never be ploughed or fertilised. The track past the hillfort and the causewayed camp is an old highway from Salisbury and there are two eighteenth-century milestones in the banks. The track plunges down the steep scarp here and becomes Long Lane, passes the Red Lion free house at a crossroads and becomes a little lane called Tower Road. A little valley to the left soon leads down to Stourhead's famous eighteenth-century landscape garden.

The route now reaches the second of three steps down to the Somerset Levels, at a point where travellers on this route have always been able to get their first sight, given clear weather, of the distinctive silhouette of Glastonbury Tor. The scarp forms a natural boundary which is marked by monuments from three very different periods.

First, an ancient earthwork follows the county boundary for 4 miles (6km) between Wiltshire and Somerset along the top of the scarp from King's Wood (ST 750358) to Gare Hill (ST 778400). It is certainly defensive with a ditch below the bank and could be Saxon, but as this feature forms the border between the settlements of the Durotriges and their tribal neighbours to the north-west, the Dobunni, it could just as well be Iron Age.

Then there is a socket from a medieval cross which marks the county boundary at a point (ST 745352) where it makes a sharp angle. This octagonal stone stands 22yd (20m) along the footpath on the north side of the lane.

Finally, and most obvious of all, is Alfred's

Tower on the other side of the lane, a folly 164ft (50m) high which was built in 1772. It is supposed to commemorate the decisive Battle of Edington in 878 when King Alfred halted the inexorable advance of the Danes. This marks the spot where the Wessex armies met up after a winter in hiding before routing their enemies near Chippenham.

Behind the cross Selwood Barrow (ST 746354) lies in a wood and is confusingly known as Jack's Castle because of its great size. Colt Hoare excavated this Bronze Age tomb in about 1805 and found 'an axe of a species of stone called Sienite. The axe is one of the most perfect we have discovered and is very nicely formed'. The lane plunges steeply down the scarp towards habitation after the long, lonely ridge from Grovely Hill. Our route follows a series of footpaths past Holland Farm, then a seventeenth-century house at Heaven Farm (ST 728359), through the hamlet of North Brewham to Goodedge Farm, then past Batt's Farm to Copplesbury Farm. From here Copplesbury Lane leads straight towards the last Iron Age feature before the Isle of Avalon itself.

Lamyatt Beacon Pagan Temple

On all our pilgrimages, pagan or Christian, there are minor shrines along the way. At Lamyatt Beacon (ST 670362) a Romano-Celtic temple and settlement called Creech Hill Camp are sited prominently on a sharp ridge. Unfortunately, treasure hunters, including the boys of nearby King's School, Bruton, have robbed the site extensively. A rescue dig found an underground chamber beside the main temple, six bronze figurines of Roman deities and several hundred coins which date the occupation to about AD250-375. Casual finds include eight small pits which were probably intended for votive offerings and two more pieces of bronze statuette described as 'two old legs'. It would be fascinating to know more about this important shrine – the inventor of the metal detector has a lot to answer for!

The only comparable site along our route is Cold Kitchen Hill, which actually has a much longer history. A late Bronze Age temple complex occupied an exposed hilltop north-east of White Sheet hillfort. There were a number of very large buildings and more than two temples, as well as a big mound and large settlement, which were in use continuously for about 1,500 years.

The past 31 miles (50km) have been littered with Iron Age remains, but they suddenly stop at Lamyatt Beacon and the last 15 miles (25km) to Glastonbury show Saxon evidence only.

Across the Somerset Levels

The long way round to Lamyatt on the lane passes the Ilchester Arms free house, but a footpath goes down from the beacon more directly. Lamyatt is a shrunken village, which explains why the hamlet is so oddly strung out. Earthworks at both ends of the village testify to the missing medieval houses, hollow ways and boundaries: there is a good view of them from the south side of the churchyard.

To reach the next village of Ditcheat, there is a footpath via Redlands Farm and a bridge over the tiny River Alham. St Mary's, Ditcheat, is a splendidly embattled building. A gabled manor house overlooks the spacious churchyard, its yew trees and the remains of a medieval cross. Inside are some fine Norman piers and a huge mural of St Christopher, the patron saint of travellers, which was first painted in the thirteenth century.

From Ditcheat the spine of Pennard Hill points straight towards Glastonbury, so it would be reasonable to expect a prehistoric causeway to have linked Lamyatt Beacon with the east end of the Pennard ridgeway. Our route follows very quiet lanes and trackways along the ridge. The only noisy interruptions are the vehicles on the A37, but perhaps we can forgive them as they too are pursuing an historic route – the Fosse Way from Bath to Ilchester. The hamlet of East Pennard gives a taste of civilised landscaping on the bare undulating ridge. The tip of Glastonbury Tor keeps dipping below the horizon, until you reach the field on the west end of Pennard Hill which offers the best view of all of the Isle of Avalon.

A footpath drops down the steep slope to West Pennard church which has a splendid late fifteenth-century cross in the churchyard. In this village our route joins a known prehistoric trackway which follows the line of the A361 from Shepton Mallet to Glastonbury.

This view towards Pennard Hill and Glastonbury Tor opens up on the last lip of the Grovely ridgeway at Creech Hill. On the left is the slope of Lamyatt Beacon (199m/653ft)

THE ISLE OF AVALON – A CELTIC PARADISE?

'We need not believe that the Glastonbury legends are records of facts; but the existence of those legends is a very great fact.'

E. A. Freeman

It would be easy to rearrange the Glastonbury myths into a new book of fantastic stories. Many people have done it and, after all, today's fantastic stories are tomorrow's ancient Glastonbury legends. Instead, here is a brief attempt to ignore the fantastic and to arrange the more credible tales into a chronological sequence.

The Spiral Maze and the Earth Goddess

Many guidebooks explain that the terraces on the side of the tor are lynchets for medieval cultivation. Twenty years ago this was hard to believe and now it is impossible to do so, for in 1966 a visitor from Ireland, Geoffrey Russell, discovered a startling fact about the arrangement of these terraces: they form a spiral path of seven complete circuits that climbs from the base to the summit of the tor. A pilgrim must therefore tread the seven to reach the top, the number seven having special significance in magic and in all ancient religions.

This spiritual pathway does not form a simple spiral, however, for it is stretched out by the elongated shape of the hill, which may account for the time it has taken to discover it. The pattern forms a spiral maze, but not a maze in the usual sense of the word where there are many choices of route, for there is only one way through and there are no side turnings. After each circuit the path turns back on itself and goes around in the opposite direction; and there are two phases in the journey where the path moves outwards before its final approach to the centre.

The spiral maze occurs elsewhere in prehistory – for example, on Cretan coins, in classical Greece, and on rock carvings at Tintagel, Cornwall, and at Hollywood, County Wicklow. The maze is usually circular in shape, but it is also found adapted to a square, semicircular or, in the case of the tor, roughly oval outline.

The interpretation of the terraces as a spiral

maze has received some academic support, unlike the more fantastic theories – such as the idea that there is a zodiac concealed in the landscape – which rely on the wishful thinking of incorrigible dreamers. Professor Philip Rahtz, who excavated the tor in the 1960s, commented that 'If the maze theory were demonstrated to be true, it would clearly be of the greatest relevance to the origins of Glastonbury as a religious centre'.

The track of the Spiral Maze encircles the centre seven times: it is elongated to fit Glastonbury Tor (Photo: author)

The Neolithic Sanctuary and the Mother Goddess

It is not known when the spiral maze was created, but the work may date back to the first worship at Glastonbury in the neolithic period and so be contemporary with the earlier phases at Avebury and Stonehenge. There is plenty of evidence to suggest the presence of neolithic settlers on the tor and in the surrounding marshes. A stone axehead and many flint flakes found by Professor Rahtz prove that men frequented the tor at that time. The timber trackways laid across the marshes show that men occupied the 'islands': the Sweet Track runs for 1½ miles (2.5km) through Shapwick Heath nature reserve and at six thousand years old is claimed to be the oldest trackway in the world.

Even before the neolithic revolution replaced nomadic hunting with a settled existence, the Mother Goddess was the most powerful deity. Statues show her in an advanced state of pregnancy with swollen breasts and very wide hips. She is an obvious symbol of human regeneration and of mankind's close relationship with the earth, the source of all bounty. Geoffrey Ashe has found

some links between the goddess and the spiral maze and has discussed them in his book *Avalonian Quest*, which introduces a degree of critical incisiveness that is so lacking in enthusiastic ramblings on the Glastonbury legends. Ashe's links and Rahtz's finds give us tantalising glimpses of the type of religious centre that might have existed on the tor in 2000BC: a shrine to the Mother Goddess approached only by seven meandering circuits around her hilltop sanctuary.

Avalon and the Celtic Underworld

Some aspects of the ancient British religion survived the Celtic invasion. So, while Stonehenge and hundreds of other stone circles were deserted in the Iron Age, Glastonbury never lost its importance as a religious centre.

In the Celtic religion the most important aspect of Glastonbury seems to have been as the entrance to the Underworld. To many people a key document is *The Life of St Collen*. A version written down by a Welsh saint in about AD650 relates the story of a Christian hermit and his journey down to the interior of the tor, but to the student of Celtic myths the tale is clearly Celtic folklore which has been given a later Christian dress. This transfer of pagan legends to the new religion occurred often – for example, the story of St Winefrede as related in Chapter 9.

Collen lived in a hermitage on the side of the tor. One day he overheard two men outside his cell say that the hill was the home of Gwyn ap Nudd, king of the fairies. Collen protested that Gwyn and the fairies were demons, but the men replied that he would soon be punished for such an insult. A messenger came and summoned Collen to climb the tor and meet Gwyn. He reluctantly agreed, took some holy water with him and entered the tor through a magic door at the summit. Within the hilltop he found King Gwyn seated on a golden throne in a splendid palace with attendants clad in red and blue. After prudently refusing a dangerous offer of fairy food, Collen scattered the holy water around him. The underground palace and its denizens disappeared and Collen found himself outside, alone on the tor.

The story of St Collen reveals the ancient belief

The summit of Glastonbury Tor, the Celtic abode of the dead, now crowned by the tower of the Archangel Michael

that the tor is a hollow hill and a point of entry into the pre-Christian Underworld. In studying the Avalon legend there seems to be a strong possibility that the Celts used the spiral maze to approach the eerie abode of their ancestors. In Celtic mythology the entrance to the land of the dead is called Avalon, a tall hill surrounded by water and guarded by a deity or king called Avallach. Geoffrey Russell linked Avalon with Caer Sidi, the spiral castle mentioned in the Welsh poem 'The Spoils of Annwn', a supernatural place where the powers inherent in death meet the energies inherent in life. Whatever Avalon meant in spiritual terms to the Celts, we have inherited a strong tradition that identifies the mythical place of Avalon with Glastonbury. And the Celtic name for Glastonbury, Ynys-witrin, the Isle of Glass, evokes a view of the island reflected in the flooded marshes which surrounded it in ancient times.

There is also the evidence of a pre-Roman earthwork called Ponter's Ball, a prominent bank just over ½ mile (1km) long, which stretches across the only ancient causeway that connects the Isle of Avalon with the outside world; it disappears suddenly into the levels at each end. Dr Ralegh Radford, an archaeologist who specialised in Glastonbury, argues that it could not have been a military defence and concludes that:

> It is most easily explicable as the *Temenos* or enclosure of a great pagan Celtic sanctuary. Analogy suggests that the focus of this sanctuary, the sacred grove or high place, must be sought near a hill beside a spring. Chalice Well, the principal spring on the island, lies immediately below the highest summit, Glastonbury Tor.

The Chalice Well

If we accept that the discovery of the spiral maze on Glastonbury Tor is evidence of a neolithic sanctuary, then it would be likely that the sacred spring known as Chalice Well has also been venerated from a very early period. It is hard to be sure, however, for the 1961 excavations around the area of the well itself found Iron Age pot sherds, but nothing of an earlier date. The Celts are well known for celebrating the magical life-sustaining properties of water at springs and streams. The

evidence shows that the Celts also worshipped a local deity at the Chalice Well, where their priests, the Druids, are said to have practised their springtime rituals. Some people think that the Druids had a college of instruction at Glastonbury – a fascinating suggestion, but one which takes us into the realm of speculation.

Chalice Well was originally called Chalk Well, or Blood Spring, because of its colour. More recently the story has grown up that the Holy Grail sought by King Arthur's knights is hidden here. In some versions of the myth, the Holy Grail is the cup, or chalice, used at the Last Supper, so that the well water assumes its colour when it mixes with Christ's blood contained in the cup. Like the blood of St Thomas at Canterbury, the blood of Jesus retains its power however much it is diluted, always colouring the water and healing those who have faith in it.

Today, the Chalice Well Trust looks after the site. Their beautiful sloping gardens are a tranquil sanctuary which exhales a spirit of peaceful contemplation. The natural chalybeate spring is now capped to maintain its purity and fills a five-sided well of medieval workmanship at the top of the garden. The spring also passes through a pipe and cascades from the mouth of a stone lion, enters Arthur's Courtyard and flows into the Pilgrim's Bath where many forms of healing have occurred. The water finds its way underground to a pool at the foot of the garden and then joins other underground streams that flow beneath the abbey grounds.

The well itself is covered by an iron lid which was designed by Frederick Bligh Bond, a Glastonbury mystic who excavated the abbey until he fell foul of the Church of England earlier this century. He chose to represent the mystical *vesica piscis* in wrought iron, an ancient symbol which represents the blending of the masculine and feminine principles, yin and yang, and the place where the conscious and unconscious worlds meet. The intersection between the two overlapping circles is the *piscis* (fish), or mandorla, a shape symbolising the female genitals which in prehistoric times were regarded as the gate of earthly existence and of spiritual knowledge.

The sacred Chalice Well on the Isle of Avalon. The wrought-iron cover incorporates the vesica piscis *symbol*

Celtic Pilgrims and the Iron Age Settlement

Who were the Celtic pilgrims that we have followed in our imagination on our journey from Old Sarum? If we knew of a large Iron Age or Romano-British cemetery on the Isle of Avalon we might think of a funeral cortège. If we had the foundations of a temple we might imagine a settlement specially built to receive religious supplicants.

What we do have from the period are the two 'lake villages' at Meare and Godney, close to the Isle of Avalon. These two groups of thatched timber dwellings that stood on the edge of pools have been studied intensively and the results of this research may be seen at the Tribunal Museum in Glastonbury High Street. Excavations, however, throw no light on the religious centre.

The religious story of Avalon continues unbroken to the present day: it includes Joseph of Arimathea's reputed visit with the infant Jesus, the possibility that the very first Christian community in Britain was here, and the development of the enormously powerful and wealthy medieval abbey with its highly influential school. But all this lies outside our chosen theme, as do the complex Arthurian legends. On the Christian period let us simply observe that it may be significant that the abbey was built on the one large site on the Isle of Avalon from which the eerie abode of Gwyn could not be seen; but the triumphant tower of the Archangel Michael, who conquered the Devil, *is* visible from there.

OLD SARUM TO GLASTONBURY

ROUTE LENGTH: 46½ miles (75km) · MAPS: OS 1:50,000 Nos 183, 184

PUBLIC HOUSES

Map ref	Name of Pub	Location
ST 970328	Black Dog***	Chilmark, 1¼ miles (2km) S of path
ST 911329	Lamb***	Hindon, 2½ miles (4km) S of path
ST 811323	Old Ship**	Mere, Castle St, 1¾ miles (3km) S of path
ST 787354	Red Lion***	Long Lane, near Kilmington
ST 775340	Spread Eagle***#	Stourton, 1 mile (1½km) S of path
ST 722362	Old Plough*	South Brewham, 500yd (½km) W of path
ST 723370	Red Lion*	North Brewham
ST 626363	Manor House Inn*	Ditcheat
ST 546386	Red Lion**	West Pennard, on A361
ST 546386	Apple Tree**	West Pennard, on A361
ST 499390	George and Pilgrims****#	Glastonbury, High Street
ST 498388	Mitre**	Glastonbury, Benedict Street
ST 504384	Rifleman's Arms**	Glastonbury, near Chalice Well

Key: ***   Highly recommended by the *Good Pub Guide*   *   Recommended
       **   Recommended by the *Good Pub Guide*   #   Accommodation

BED & BREAKFAST ACCOMMODATION

Map ref	Name of House	Location/Telephone number
SU 135295	Old Mill Hotel†	Town Path, West Harnham, near Salisbury. Tel: (0722) 27517
ST 870450	West House	West Street, Warminster, 5 miles (8km) N of path. Tel: (0985) 213936
ST 870450	Tudor House	West Street, Warminster, 5 miles (8km) N of path. Tel: (0985) 215054
ST 775340	Spread Eagle	Church Lawn, Stourton, 1 mile (1½km) S of path. Tel: (0747) 840587
ST 499390	George and Pilgrims‡	High Street, Glastonbury. Tel: (0458) 31146

Key: †   From here John Constable painted his famous picture of Salisbury Cathedral.
      ‡   Built to accommodate pilgrims by John of Selwood, abbot of Glastonbury in the 1470s.

NB: This is by no means an exhaustive list of accommodation, but all are historic buildings off the beaten track; some are expensive.

PUBLIC TELEPHONES

Map ref	Location of Telephone
SU 092321	Wilton to Great Wishford lane, S of railway bridge
SU 049363	Little Langford, below Grovely Castle
SU 033369	Hanging Langford, below East Castle
SU 027320	Baverstock, S of Hanging Langford Camp
	NB: A303: none closer than 2½ miles (4km) in either direction on this road
ST 863387	Brixton Deverill, NW of Pertwood Down
ST 598375	East Pennard, by bridge

NB: There are several call-boxes in larger places such as Mere and Wilton; generally, one may be found outside a post office. During reasonable hours it is possible to telephone from the pubs listed above.

VILLAGES OR HAMLETS WITH GENERAL STORES

Salisbury, Wilton, South Newton, Wylye, Stockton, Chicklade (café on A303), Kingston Deverill, Mere, South Brewham, Lamyatt, Ditcheat, West Pennard, Glastonbury.

TOURIST INFORMATION OFFICES

Salisbury, Warminster, Mere, Stourton (National Trust), Wincanton, Glastonbury.

2

THE WATERS
OF THE GAP

I f you make a pilgrimage from England to Rome along the road that was used during the Middle Ages, you will follow a direct Roman road from the Channel ports to the Alps. At one stage, after you leave Châlons-sur-Marne in the direction of Bar-sur-Aube, you will find yourself walking along the best-preserved length (about 25 miles/40km) of Roman road in the whole of Gaul. It makes magnificent walking through prosperous farmland, the surface paved today with the fine chalk rubble its builders used. Some long-forgotten historical accident, the destruction of a bridge perhaps, has caused this major long-distance route to move its actual line sideways, leaving the old road in merely local use by farmers.

It is a common story, repeated in Britain on the Fosse Way south of Cirencester. The result is a blessing to modern walkers. You might explore the entire network of Roman roads in Britain using the Ordnance Survey's *Map of Roman Britain*, but you will never find a better stretch to walk than this.

If you look at the modern OS map (sheet numbers 163 and 173 at a scale of 1:50,000), even if all the writing were magically removed, you could still identify this feature as a Roman road on three counts. First, it is straight for long stretches (in one place 16¾ miles/27km), only changing its alignment on a ridge where the original surveyors had a good view. Secondly, early medieval boundaries follow it all the way, so in Saxon times it must have already existed as an important feature in the landscape.

Thirdly, it has that peculiar status among English rights of way, a 'byway open to all traffic', which shows that it is both wider than a bridleway and hallowed by travellers over the centuries. Un-fortunately, a few short stretches have been spoiled by a small group using it as a cross-country track for their jeeps. This is to the detriment of the fabric of the Fosse Way (a steep bank south of Tetbury has been churned up to become 2ft deep mud), and to its other users.

Britain's leading investigator of Roman roads, the late Ivan Margary, so loved this 'footpath' section that he used an aerial photograph of it as the frontispiece to his book *Roman Roads in Britain*.

· THE FOSSE WAY ·

The Fosse Way as a Frontier
The Fosse Way, when complete, ran all the way from Topsham, near Exeter, via Cirencester (Corinium) and Leicester (Ratae) to Lincoln (Lindum). As the oldest section ran from Cirencester to Lincoln, it is easy to regard the Fosse Way as the earliest frontier along a natural divide between lowland and upland Britain along a convenient line from the Severn to the Humber estuary. Certainly by AD47 Roman garrisons or friendly kings controlled all the lowlands of south and east England, and we know of early forts that were actually on the Fosse Way – for example, at its terminus in Cirencester. But detailed evidence shows that the Fosse Way was not a definite boundary like Hadrian's Wall in the following century, but was more of a frontier zone.

To establish such a useful lateral road as the Fosse Way, that linked the radial roads from London to all quarters of the new province, it would have been necessary to enjoy strong control over the country to the north and west of the route. In other words, such Midlands forts as Wroxeter provided the security for building and operating the Fosse Way safely. Behind this line the Romanisation of the country could proceed apace and quickly provide an income for the empire, whereas beyond it in the highland zone the invaders saw only diminishing returns in the face of hostile mountain tribes like the Brigantes in the Pennines and the Silures of South Wales.

The reason for the Fosse Way's early terminus at Cirencester may have been that Vespasian had conquered the Dumnonii of Devon and Cornwall and so secured the province's south-west flank. Cirencester would in its early days have been an important junction, with the heaviest traffic coming up the Ermin Way from the Dorset ports to supply the forward units of the army.

Roman Travellers and Engineering

Although the Roman engineers built some roads through mountainous country which were wide enough only for mule trains, they intended all new roads in Britain for wheeled traffic from the start. Vehicles included the *plaustrum*, the ordinary wooden cart; the *carpentum*, the fast two-wheeled van used by the imperial post; and the *carruca*, a heavy luxury carriage. It is said that it was possible to rest, converse or dictate letters in a *carruca* (although it apparently had no springs) and Julius Caesar is reputed to have written a book in a carriage while he crossed the Alps.

The Romans built their vehicles to a standard wheel-gauge of 42-3in (1,070-1,100mm) and the roads were constructed to suit this width of vehicle. But the four-wheelers, whether they were heavy, lumbering freight waggons or luxury carriages, had one thing in common – they had no steering. Brute force had to be used therefore to manoeuvre them around corners, so the Roman engineers had to build their roads with gentle curves, that would not present the drivers of four-wheeled vehicles with steering problems.

If the bends were leisurely the gradients were extremely steep. A Roman road, such as the famous paved stretch over the Pennines which survives at Blackstone Edge, near Halifax, ascends directly up a slope, unlike a modern road which would be constructed with hairpin bends to lessen the gradient. The Romans would have built their road directly

The pediment of the Temple of Sulis at Bath. The head of the goddess appears in the centre, wreathed in snakes

up the steep banks of the Cotswold streams on the Fosse Way; a deviation along an easier gradient, such as on the south side of the River Avon, indicates a modification built during the Middle Ages.

Books often show a cross-section of a Roman road to illustrate their method of construction. Such drawings are grossly misleading, because they imply that the same type of road was built all over the Roman Empire, whereas the reverse is true. The Roman engineers varied their technique widely according to the nature of the ground, the gradients and the expected traffic. Across marshy ground they would begin with a causeway of logs, like the *toghers* laid across the peat in prehistoric Ireland or across the Somerset Levels to the 'island' of Glastonbury; on firmer soil a stable bank called an *agger* was constructed of carefully graded layers of well-compacted stones to form a stable, self-draining foundation. Paving stones were used only in towns where heavy traffic was expected, or on steep slopes where a firm footing was needed. Alongside precipices a common practice was to cut wheel grooves to prevent vehicles from slipping sideways into the abyss.

The most common and least costly surface was a layer of gravel or fine chalk rubble, which makes a surprisingly durable road. This surface was probably used on the Fosse Way. Although you will occasionally see traces of paving slabs half-buried in the mud, it is hard to say how old they might be, or indeed what they might be – they could even be drain covers. Excavations in Long Newnton parish for a waterworks trench in 1961 along the middle of the Fosse Way revealed 'a layer of stones three to four inches thick covered by one inch of small stone chips' and 'the agger showed no signs of heavy wear or repair' (Ordnance Survey records). Archaeologists examined another cross-section of the Fosse Way at the north end of the green road in Culkerton Wood (close to RAF Kemble Airfield) and discovered that construction was of alternate layers of limestone flags and gravelly sand, with rammed sand and gravel in the centre. The metalling of the roadway was 18ft 10in (574cm) wide (Bristol & Gloucestershire Archaeological Society Transactions, Vol 611).

The Roman City of Corinium:
Britannia's Second City

Although today Cirencester thinks of itself as the head of the Cotswold district, in Roman times it was much more important, for it rose to become the island's second largest city after London, and the wealthy capital of Britannia Prima, a province embracing all of Wales and Wessex.

Military strategists chose the site of Corinium soon after Claudius invaded Britain in AD43: it lay at a good crossing point of the River Churn during their westwards advance. It became both a legionary and cavalry station that was well placed to act as a supply base for the forward forts along the Welsh border. From here five main roads radiate, so supplies coming up from the Dorset ports could be dispatched north, east or west. By AD60 this role was over, the barracks were demolished and the civilian settlement flourished in their stead.

Corinium, also called Corinium Dobunnorum after the surrounding Celtic tribe, became a *civitas*, or town of local importance, and soon acquired all the trappings of Roman civic pride. The symbol of Roman administration was a splendid *basilica*, 335ft (102m) long and 96ft (29m) wide, in the centre of town. The early Christians copied this type of building for their churches and purloined the name, but to a Roman civilian a basilica meant a town hall and law court combined – at Corinium it was lined with marble and boasted a 90ft (27m) diameter

apse at one end for the judicial throne.

Although none of the actual sites are known for certain, finds of pipework, heated rooms and sculpture show that the town possessed an aqueduct, piped water supplies, at least one heated bathing establishment and several temples. The public buildings and houses occupied thirty *insulae*, or blocks of land, which were defined by the square grid of streets within the city walls – a total of 250 acres (101ha).

The forum occupied the central insula at the crossing of the two axial streets, the Fosse Way and Ermin Way. The magnificent scale of the facilities, measuring 550 × 360ft (168 × 110m), and the monumental buildings must have overawed the native Celts. The basilica lay on the south-east, while a range of shops stretched around the other three sides, with splendid colonnades facing both inwards to the piazza and outwards onto the surrounding streets. A forum for butchers has been found nearby: the existence of such specialised markets indicates that commerce in Corinium was on an exceptionally large scale by the standards of Roman Britain. The surplus wealth encouraged craftsmen, and we know of flourishing workshops of sculptors and metalworkers. But perhaps the most telling sign of the city's prosperity is the famous Corinium mosaic school, one of the major mosaic workshops of the western empire. Mosaic floors were laid in at least fifty villas, some as far away as Oxfordshire and Somerset. Six Corinium houses show mosaic work: this may not seem a large number, but only 1 per cent of the Roman town has been excavated.

Description of the Walk

The Fosse Way may leave the Roman town of Corinium (Cirencester) on the line of modern Castle Street, passing the presumed site of a Roman gateway at the junction with Park Lane and then leading directly south-west along the line of the Tetbury Road, the A433. This forms a straight alignment with the Tetbury Road, but not with the Fosse Way that enters from the other side of town along modern Lewis Lane. It is puzzling that the main road should leave from the north end and not from the centre of the Roman town, involving two

WATERS·OF·THE
CIRENCESTER·TO·BA

SHERSTON

ALDERTON

M4
ROMANO BRITISH DITCH
AND POTTERY FOUND
? ROMAN COFFIN FOUND
BURTON
LITTLETON DREW
LUGBURY LONG BARROW
THE SALUTATION
PH
GRITTLETON
NETTLETON SHRINE OF APOLLO
MOTTE AND BAILEY
CASTLE COMBE
ROMAN COIN HOARD AND
SITE OF ROMAN BUILDING
M4
FOSSE WAY
MARSHFIELD
SITE AND REMAINS OF NORTH
WRAXALL ROMAN VILLA
THE SHOE PH
SITE OF ROMAN BUILDING
C2-C4 POTTERY
ROMAN COFFIN BURIALS
ROMAN COINS, BROOCH
AND SHERD FOUND
ROMAN COIN HOARD AND
POSSIBLE ROMAN SITES
COLERNE
ROMAN VILLA
REMAINS OF ROMAN BUILDING
THREE SHIRES
STONE
REMAINS OF ROMAN BUILDING
A4
LITTLE SOLSBURY HILL FORT
(Iron Age)
? ROMAN EARTHENWARE FOUND
BATHEASTON
AQVAE SVLIS
FOSSE WAY
ROMAN BURIAL
(BATH)
BATHAMPTON
A4
ROMAN COIN FOUND
CORSHAM
BATHFORD
SHRINE AND BATHS COMPLEX
ROMAN OCCUPATION SITES
BATHAMPTON DOWN HILL FORT
(Iron Age)
SITE OF ROMAN BUILDINGS
FOSSE WAY (A367)
A36
KILOMETRES
MILES

GAP
H

CORINIVM
(CIRENCESTER)

ERMIN WAY (A417)

FOSSE WAY (A424)

ROMAN WALLS

RODMARTON ◦○ HOCBERRY ROMAN VILLA

FOSSE WAY (A429)

AMPHITHEATRE   FORUM

A 433

JACKAMENTS
BOTTOM

■ THAMES HEAD PH

CULKERTON

KEMBLE ‐ AIRFIELD

■ TETBURY   ROMANO‐   ■ ASHLEY   ■ KEMBLE
  BRITISH OCCUPATION SITE ○

            ROMAN SETTLEMENT ○
              Addy's Firs
LONG NEWNTON ■
            ROMAN SETTLEMENT ○
              Ashley Marsh Court
                                                    ■ POOLE KEYNES
     ROMAN SETTLEMENT ○
       Newnton Farm   ○ ROMANO‐BRITISH OCCUPATION SITE
                             Chedglow Barn
FOSSE WAY
                              ■ CRUDWELL
■ SHIPTON MOYNE

UPPOSED ROMAN
ITE
rt   ERMIN WAY (A419)
  ■ EASTON GREY
  ○ ROMAN "DISCUS" FOUND
EARTHWORK ○
      ◦ ROMAN VICUS
       "White walls" at Avon crossing

■ MALMESBURY
  Abbey

+ NORTON
  ROMAN URN FOUND

■ HALLAVINGTON
  ROMAN COINS FOUND

right-angle turns for a traveller wanting to pass through Cirencester on the Fosse Way.

So it is possible that we would be more correct to leave on the Via Principalis from the main Roman intersection, a street now called Querns Lane. Where this passes through the line of the Roman city wall, mechanical excavations in 1975 revealed the foundations of a south-west gate, but whether this was for the Fosse Way or merely for access to the impressive amphitheatre outside the city walls, it is hard to say. It is worth visiting the huge oval earth banks of the amphitheatre – despite all the re-development on this side of Cirencester and the close proximity of the so-called Phoenix Way, once you are standing inside its peaceful 'ramparts' it still preserves the feeling that it stands in the countryside outside the town. If the road to the amphitheatre was really the Fosse Way, then its line must bend north around the embankments and join up with the Tetbury Road in about half a mile.

The Tetbury Road today is a fine highway, generally raised up by 4-5ft (1.2-1.5m) above the surrounding land, and sometimes by as much as 6ft (1.8m). Towards Jackaments Bottom a deep hollow runs along the south side of the road. These features are thought to represent surviving Roman engineering on a grand scale. There is plenty of space to walk along the verges, but it is the busy main road from Cirencester to Tetbury and not a peaceful stroll.

However, two points of interest divert our attention after 3 miles (5km). A signposted footpath on the right runs parallel to the remains of the eighteenth-century Thames and Severn Canal (disused since 1927), reaching in a few hundred yards the source of the River Thames at ST 980994. Surprisingly, the combe is dry and only in flood conditions does the spring gush forth here. On the site once stood a splendid neo-Roman stone head symbolising Old Father Thames. Unfortunately, the colossal sculpture became so vandalised in this remote spot that its remains were shifted in 1974 to the nearby Thames Head pub. This watering hole on the main road at ST 981987 is the second source of relief from the traffic on the A433 and the landlord will relate the story of the river's source.

It is clear from the Ordnance Survey map that the Fosse Way descends Jackaments Bottom and then picks up a new alignment at ST 965976 where the A433 Tetbury Road veers off. The Roman road climbed the steep slope back up onto the Cotswold plateau where it crosses Kemble Airfield. Rather than trespass on RAF property, we must make a detour using a dismantled railway line as far as the hamlet of Culkerton, then climbing back up a pretty lane to the Fosse Way at ST 947952.

The Green Road Section
This is where the wonderful Fosse Way walk really begins – one of the most interesting green roads in the south of England. If your object is to explore a half-abandoned stretch of Roman road rather than to travel all the way to Bath, then the best section to walk along begins at RAF Kemble and ends either at the Lordswood Farm crossroads (ST 872843, 8¼ miles/13.2km), or at the Salutation public house by a crossroads called the Gibb under Gatcombe Hill (ST 837792, 12¼ miles/ 19.7km). Both spots make a good rendezvous if you want to avoid retracing your steps.

The going is generally good, but in winter parts can be muddy due mostly to the passage of essential farm vehicles. Despite the passing of two thousand years, the Roman drainage still works. Only in one place has it failed: on the slope approaching the Lordswood crossroads the land drains out along the Fosse Way. So here – and it *was* November after a snowstorm – we had to leave the Roman road, crossing the boundary hedge into adjacent fields. In summer, however, walkers will encounter no such problems. And, if the rider is prepared to stop and clean out the mudguards every few miles, it should be easily negotiable on a bicycle – in fact, very good fun.

The course of the Fosse Way is absolutely straight for the next 16¾ miles (27km); occasional tiny deviations occur in crossing watercourses, but they always rejoin the original alignment. Thomas Codrington suggested early in this century that the surveyors laid out the line from the high ground in Cirencester Park a mile west of the town. As you top each rise it is possible to look back and see this 500ft (145m) ridge, called Pope's Seat, at the end of the alignment. Codrington, incidentally, explored this section in a two-wheeled 'dog-cart'.

The track crosses a plateau of gently rolling arable farmland. On each side of the raised road is a prominent bank and a hedge, often as high as 12ft (3.6m). Sometimes the whole space between the hedges is clear greensward and invading seedlings are crushed by walkers' boots or tractors' wheels; at other places small trees and undergrowth have invaded the space of the roadway so that the footpath winds among the scrub and it is hard to see very far ahead, despite the straightness of the hedges. The muddiness of the surface depends on the width, gradient, season and amount of use, or indeed abuse, by motorised vehicles.

The variation in width across the agger, or hedges, is curious in that it seems to follow no rational pattern: it is often 60ft (18m) wide for long lengths, then it will contract to a steady 30ft (9m), occasionally narrowing to as little as 18ft (5.4m). Where the agger is visible it is from 2-5ft (0.6-1.5m) high with a slope on either side of about 1 in 5 down to the general level of the fields. Often it is worn away or silted up and only the hedges mark the original boundaries of the highway. The agger is particularly prominent on the green section a little north of Fosse Gate at ST 943946, where it is 33ft (10m) wide and 4ft (1.2m) high.

Apart from the interruption at RAF Kemble,

there is only one obstruction all the way to Bath. After crossing the infant River Avon near Foxley the road disappears for ½ mile (800m), although it is marked on the map as a 'byway open to all traffic' and on the ground by the line of a single hedge. As the rule is 'straight on', it would be difficult to lose your way even here. It is possible that the Fosse Way did actually make a local detour here to avoid some wet ground, and this detour may be connected with a branch road that the Romans made through Easton Grey north-west to the River Severn at Arlingham, probably for the iron mines in the Forest of Dean.

The Gloucestershire/Wiltshire county boundary follows the Fosse Way from the top of the scarp at Jackaments Bottom to the parish of Easton Grey, some 11 miles (18km) in all. Old parish boundaries often coincide with our route as well and help to confirm its antiquity.

The Saxons habitually placed their settlements slightly away from the main roads they inherited from the Romans, a safety measure which is abundantly clear on this route. Often the most you see of a village is the church spire or tower a mile or

A typical view along the green road section of the Fosse Way. The width of the agger at this point is about 60ft, but trees and scrub have grown in from the ditches

This pretty Cotswold bridge crosses the infant River Avon on the exact line of the Fosse Way. The Roman road originally went straight up the steep bank on the right

two from the Fosse Way, as with Tetbury, Long Newnton and Sherston. Good views open out often, but usually you must reach a gate to see them because of the high hedges – for example, the gate to the disused airfield near Newnton House (ST 924921) where a prospect of Malmesbury Abbey is revealed with Marlborough Downs in the distance.

Although people and houses are rare along this green way, there are plenty of curiosities to divert those who look hard enough. Most of the Roman sites near the Fosse Way are shown on our map. The information on these buildings, and the find spots of coins, urns and other archaeological material comes from the records of the Royal Commission on Historical Monuments. Of course, there is little to see on most of the sites, but at the Romano-British settlement site near Ashley March Covert (ST 930930) sandstone roofing tile fragments about ⅓in (1cm) thick are numerous in the plough-soil.

The most important site that we pass in this section is White Walls, a major Roman settlement, undefended but substantial, on the north bank of the River Avon at ST 890872. Some researchers have identified it with the Roman place-name *Mutuantonis*, which was taken from the classical Ravenna Cosmography, but this is not certain. The Ordnance Survey removed the Roman name from their maps in 1923. If you ask permission from the farmer who owns the land you can investigate a flat circular occupation mound in White Walls Wood at the top of the bank: it is about 150yd (137m) in diameter with entrances on the north and south sides. Although this site commands a good view of the river crossing, which is now marked by a pretty Cotswold stone bridge with three arches, it is unexcavated. It could be either a military camp associated with the Roman *vicus*, or it could be a long-forgotten medieval moat. Sir Richard Colt Hoare, the Wiltshire antiquary who wrote in 1821, mentions Roman foundations and tessellated pavements in the valley at White Walls. The natural site for the settlement would be the bluff near the wood, which is well clear of the flood plain. Many

Roman coins, some pottery and two fragments of sculpture have turned up over the past 250 years, and show that men occupied the site from the first to the fourth centuries AD. The finds are scattered between the Malmesbury, Devizes and Ashmolean museums.

Just as curious, perhaps, is the collection of low buildings with a water tower between the White Walls Wood and the Fosse Way, which was a World War II prisoner-of-war camp. If you ask the farmer to show you around the buildings, you will see the ceiling of the former chapel-cum-dining-room, which was beautifully painted by Italian prisoners-of-war and is now used as a workshop. A splendid collection of old lorries and tractors, simply waiting for attention, lies scattered around the site.

At the Lordswood Farm crossroads the Fosse Way becomes what Codrington called a 'parish highway'. The agger here is very wide and the narrow strip of metalling snakes in a picturesque line between the straight hedges, reminding us of the way that heavy carts had to wend their way around the pot-holes in the days before the turnpike roads. While bearing the character of a country lane, the Fosse Way crosses a cutting, taking the Great Western Railway towards Bristol, but after 2¼ miles (3.6km) it reverts to a green road for another mile before tunnelling under the M4 motorway to the Salutation, the first pub for 13 miles (21km).

The Country Lane Section

From the Salutation inn, the character of the Fosse Way begins to change, though at first this is only in the surfacing and not in the size of the road. For many miles still it remains a beautiful country lane with little motor traffic.

After crossing the Chipping Sodbury to Chippenham road the Fosse Way plunges down Gatcombe Hill through a wood to cross the By Brook, climbing the other side with a slight deviation which eases the gradient. Once back on the plateau there are two antiquities to visit close to the Fosse Way, but neither of them are Roman.

On the right at ST 831786 lies Lugbury long barrow, which is visible from the lane and accessi-ble by a bridleway. It is a prehistoric burial mound, once 180 × 90ft (55 × 27m), but now, thanks to ploughing, only 6ft (1.8m) high with none of the original ditch visible. Nineteenth-century excavations found three chambers with a multiple burial of adults and children of both sexes, as well as a rifled chamber. At the east end two upright megaliths represent a false entrance that was made either to fool grave robbers or to form a setting for pagan rituals.

On the left at ST 838778 stand the impressive ruins of Castle Combe, which are accessible along a footpath from opposite Lugbury barrow which crosses to the left bank of the By Brook. The de Dunstanville family were rebellious barons who built it in about 1140 during the civil wars of King Stephen's reign. The motte, or mound, is crowned by the remains of a shell keep and has no less than four baileys, or surrounding courtyards full of buildings, each defended by a rampart of coarse masonry and rubble. The village of Castle Combe is a good place for rest and recuperation, but its prettiness is so famous that you might find the crowds of tourists who visit it overwhelming after the tranquillity of the Fosse Way.

Nettleton Temple of Apollo

Only a mile further along the Fosse Way after Castle Combe is the most important Roman settlement we shall encounter en route to Aquae Sulis. The Nettleton Temple of Apollo stood in a copse on the south bank of the Broadmead Brook, a tributary of the By Brook. Here we have a sub-sidiary pagan shrine on the Roman road that took pilgrims from the large city of Corinium to the major sacred spring at Aquae Sulis – reminiscent of the wayside crosses and pilgrim chapels that were erected on the way to important Christian shrines during the Middle Ages.

In building the Temple of Apollo, it seems likely that the Romans took over a local native cult, and, judging from the temple's position in an evocative little valley, it would seem that a Celtic water god or goddess dwelt here. (The Celtic religion and its water cults are discussed on p43 and pp133-6.)

This part of Roman Britain was heavily populated

Romans at the Nettleton shrine of Apollo, based on the excavations by the late W. J. Wedlake

and prosperous, so it is not surprising that several temples are known: more are doubtless awaiting discovery or recognition for what they are. The late W. J. Wedlake devoted a large part of his life to their study, excavating first the temple at Camerton on the Fosse Way south-west of Bath. We also know of temples at Chedworth in Gloucestershire and at Box on a limestone bluff in Wiltshire just east of Bath. Both of these structures were until recently thought to have been simply more elaborate villas than most of those in the district, but the archaeologist Graham Webster has now produced a compelling theory about their religious significance. The most fascinating finds at Box are a sculpture of Neptune (the sea god on a hilltop) and what appears to be the silver eye of a cult statue.

Bill Wedlake spent many seasons excavating the site of the Nettleton temple and its associated settlement by the brook. In his report – a massive book published by the Society of Antiquaries in 1982 – he described the temple as 'a place of pilgrimage in Roman times and a well-planned shrine set in a delectable Cotswold valley'. Our reconstruction is based on his meticulous work. The viewpoint is the modern footpath (ST 822770) on the north side of the Broadmead Brook, which in Roman times flowed in a straight artificial channel slightly south of the present stream. The platform under the octagonal temple lies now in Wick Wood, while the associated buildings shown on the left lay on the eastern fringe of the wood. The rest of the settlement occupied the whole of the water-meadow further east – that is, the whole field, which is about 500ft (152m) long between the wood and the Fosse Way.

The Temple of Apollo was established and developed continuously over the period AD69-370

– there was a post-shrine homestead on the site from 370 to 392. Nettleton was for three centuries a settlement dependent on the shrine and its many visitors and only became agricultural during the last few decades of the Roman occupation.

Among the numerous irregularly placed buildings Wedlake found evidence of pewter casting and other metal working. Clearly, local artisans were making votive offerings, as there was a special stone votive pit in the inner wall of the temple. The shrine yielded many intricate bronze brooches and a remarkable bronze votive plaque 4in (10cm) high, dedicated by one Decimius to Apollo and showing the god himself in an architectural frame – a powerful image of native workmanship. These finds are in Bristol City Museum.

The lane crosses the Broadmead Brook on a pretty bridge on the exact site of the Roman crossing, and the smooth left turn 500ft (153m) south of the stream is also a Roman bend. To the east of this bend lay a triangular camp in the first century AD, perhaps used by the army during the building of the Fosse Way, and three small cemeteries. The temple site lies on the Badminton estate and is the property of the Duke of Beaufort.

Country Lanes and Paths into Bath

The Fosse Way continues for another 3½ miles (5.6km) with much the same rural byway character as before, the roadway wandering about between straight hedges 60ft (18m) apart. The only building right on the road is Fosse Farm. At the next crossroads the first change in alignment for 16¾ miles (27km) takes place, with a turn of a few degrees to the south. Shortly afterwards the road reaches the third pub on the Fosse Way, the Shoe, at the crossroads with the A420 from Bristol to Chippenham. This early twentieth-century Cotswold stone hostelry decorated in Jacobean style serves bar meals. Soon after the Shoe inn, the road weaves a little to cross the Doncombe Brook before a second change of alignment across the last stretch of downs.

Although there is little to see on the downs, away from the Fosse Way to the left are the foundations of two Roman villas. At North Wraxall (ST 837761) on the north side of Truckle Hill are

the only traces of any Roman stonework on a Wiltshire villa, while within the bounds of the old Copenacre airfield lies the site of Colerne Roman villa. Even if anything remained you would need permission from the commanding officer to view the site, for the airfield is now the Royal Navy Stores Depot Copenacre (Colerne). Our map shows other evidence of Roman activity on this part of the plateau.

The stores depot has an unfortunate effect on the quality of the walking, for beyond its gates the character of the road changes dramatically. The tarmac is now wider, smoother and straight (for the first time). Then the traffic from the villages of Ford and Colerne merges and the Fosse Way becomes a useful B road into Bath. But the Roman engineers can take all this in their stride, for the agger is at its most impressive here as it approaches Banner Down, striding across the high plateau on a 5-6ft (1.5-1.8m) bank, with room for wide springy verges either side of the two-lane strip of bitumen.

After passing the airfield, landscaped parkland with two fine sets of entrance gates abuts the Fosse Way on the right. Look carefully where the park

The eighteenth-century Three Shires Stone stood in Gloucestershire, Somerset and Wiltshire respectively: locals converted them into this pseudo-cromlech in 1858

The view down into the Avon valley towards Aquae Sulis (Bath) fom the Fosse Way on Banner Down

wall suddenly bends away to the west (ST 796701), for here is a most unusual if not unique monument. The Three Shire Stones mark the spot where Gloucestershire, Somerset and Wiltshire all met before their boundaries were altered in the early 1970s. Initially three stones were set up, each bearing the date 1736 and the initial letter of its county. Then in 1858 a group of local gentlemen appealed for money to convert the stones into a sham cromlech or megalithic tomb with a specially quarried capstone. Visitors to a geniune ancient tomb, such as at Kit's Coty House on the North Downs in Kent (close to the Pilgrims' Way), will not be deceived for an instant: in particular, the uprights taper too closely together so that there is insufficient space within for a burial chamber. To add piquancy to the tale, these jovial gentlemen, in digging a new hole to reposition the Gloucestershire upright, came upon three skeletons and a James II coin.

Soon after the Three Shire Stones are passed, the Fosse Way reaches its highest point (620ft/189m), before beginning the steep plunge into the Avon Valley at the village of Batheaston. This is not another Avon (an old British word meaning river), but the same river returning on itself, though much larger than it was at White Walls. Look for a left turn called Morris Lane which descends steeply down the escarpment. This is followed by an old parish boundary and is therefore the more probable line of the Fosse Way. The rival claimant is the larger road known as Fosse Lane to the west.

From here the Fosse Way follows the A4, the old London turnpike along the north side of the river into Bath. As this is much too busy for pleasant walking, our route deviates to the other side of the river and follows the towpath of a picturesque stretch of the Kennet and Avon Canal into the town. To reach the towpath, turn left at the bottom of Morris Lane, pass the roundabout, climb the railway embankment, and you will find a footpath alongside the old GWR tracks high above the placid waters. The path crosses a meadow, then a branch-line level-crossing to reach the canal at Bathampton parish church and the excellent waterside pub, the George, a great favourite with narrow-boat crews. If they are too rowdy, Bathampton Mills is a very smart pub and restaurant conversion nearby which overlooks the Avon weir and a pretty Gothic toll-bridge.

The views from the canal towpath are lovely as it contours along the valley into Bath about 45ft (14m) above the river. This is certainly the quietest as well as the most picturesque way to enter Bath, or Aquae Sulis, as we must now call it.

· THE SHRINE AT AQUAE SULIS ·

The Celtic Religion

The Celtic religion centred around the worship of nature at places where she was especially bountiful or mysterious – this is reflected in the popular image of Druids worshipping in oak groves rich with mistletoe rather than in man-made temples. Of all nature's bounties, water was the most vital, and so water cults became common at springs or beside brooks. The hot spring at Bath, which is unique in Britain and wonderfully copious, excited the Celts' veneration, and this is confirmed by the discovery of coins thrown into the spring.

Here dwelt the goddess Sul, the spring a focal point where the supernatural world was thought to meet the earthly world. Here the Celts believed that they had access to the unlimited power of the supernatural. The supernatural was effective – a seething and dynamic source of energy and life, a realm rich with all possible benefits as well as perils. The coins are evidence of the powerful attraction of Aquae Sulis for the Celts, and we may assume that it was a main centre of pilgrimage centuries before the Romans invaded Britain.

Roman Development of the Sacred Spring

It was Roman imperial policy to tolerate local religions as long as the natives gave lip-service to the official cult of emperor-worship. To make the provincial shrines accessible to the settlers, the native gods were identified with the nearest equivalent Roman deity. Indeed, the process of assimilation went further at Bath than anywhere else in Britain – for example, the Britons inscribed their offerings to Sul, while the newcomers venerated her as Minerva.

Some of the votive inscriptions that were cast into the spring show everyday life in the Roman world in a dramatic light. They take the form of in-scribed lead sheets, rolled up to make the curse a secret pact between plaintiff and god, before being consigned to the mysterious steaming pool:

> May he who carried off Vilbia from me become as liquid as water. May she who obscenely devoured her become dumb whether Velvinna Exsupereus Verianus, Sevrinus Augustalis, Comitianus Catus-mininus, Germanilla or Jovina.

> I have given to Minerva the goddess Sulis the thief who has stolen my hooded cloak whether slave or free whether man or woman. He is not to redeem this offering unless with his blood.

> Docimedis has lost two gloves. He asks that the person who has stolen them should lose his mind and his eyes in the temple where she appoints.

The Celtic spring sacred to Sulis. Roman and native supplicants are seen casting their votive offerings or their curses into the depths

Roman engineers transformed the rude spring into a great ornamental pool that was rich with statues and enclosed in a grand building within a splendid precinct. They built a temple of typical Mediterranean type, with an open-air altar in front of the raised colonnade. Sculpture filled the pediment, showing in relief tritons and a (male) Medusa conflated with the native (female) Sul. The priests surrounded the temple and spring with a magnificent suite of baths so that shrine and facilities for its visitors dominated the little town, in the same way that the shrine of Our Lady dominates Lourdes today.

Life in Aquae Sulis

There is little archaeological evidence to enable us to reconstruct the social round of the pilgrims.

Roman travellers on the Fosse Way, based on a coach shown on a tomb relief now on Maria Saal Church, near Klagenfurt, Austria

Visits would have been made to the baths, temple and theatre, where both ceremonies and entertainments would have been staged. There must have been inns for the comfort of travellers, but we know nothing of the taverns or other amusement facilities.

It is unlikely that the sanctuary and the town were ever deliberately destroyed. After the withdrawal of the legions the natives gradually abandoned the place, and this may have been accelerated by the battles in the area between the Britons and the invading Saxons. In any case, once the efficient Roman drainage system was blocked the town would have flooded each time the Avon was in spate, with a consequent rapid accumulation of silt over the low-lying temple precinct. That the site was quickly buried is confirmed by the survival of the valuable lead lining to the main bath, the only place in the Roman Empire where this happened.

THE WATERS OF THE GAP: CIRENCESTER TO BATH

ROUTE LENGTH: 32½ miles (52.5km) · MAPS: OS 1:50,000 Nos 163, 172, 173

PUBLIC HOUSES

Map ref	Name of Pub	Location
SP 023020	Black Horse***#	Castle Street, Cirencester
SP 023020	Corinium Court***#	Dollar Street, Cirencester
SP 023020	Fleece***#	Market Place, Cirencester
ST 981987	Thames Head*	A433, near source of River Thames
ST 893933	Gentle Gardener***#	Long Street, Tetbury, 1.8 miles (3km) W of path
ST 933874	Old Bell***#	Abbey Row, Malmesbury, 2.4 miles (4km) E of path
ST 933874	King's Arms***#	High Street, Malmesbury, 2.4 miles (4km) E of path
ST 831804	The Plough**	Littleton Drew, ½ mile (1km) W of path
ST 838791	The Salutation**	The Gibb, on B4039 at Fosse Way
ST 843771	Castle***#	Castle Combe, 1¼ miles (2km) E of path
ST 807743	The Shoe*	A420 at Fosse Way, near Upper Wraxall
ST 787669	Crown**	Bathford Hill, Bathford
ST 774669	Bathampton Mills*	Bathampton, by River Avon weir
ST 775665	George**	Mill Lane, Bathampton, on Kennet and Avon Canal
ST 753646	Pratt's Hotel*#	South Parade, Bath
ST 751646	Crystal Palace**	Abbey Green, Bath

Key: *** Highly recommended by the *Good Pub Guide*   * Recommended
        ** Recommended by the *Good Pub Guide*   # Accommodation

BED & BREAKFAST ACCOMMODATION

Map ref	Name of House	Location/Telephone number
ST 860800	Church House	Grittleton, N side of M4. Tel: (0249) 782562
ST 745643	Oldfields	102 Wells Road, Bath. Tel: (0225) 317984
ST 794666	The Orchard	Bathford, near Bath. Tel: (0225) 858765
ST 747642	Paradise House	88 Holloway, Bath. Tel: (0225) 317723
ST 760648	Somerset House	35 Bathwick Hill, Bath. Tel: (0225) 664451

These are all smart houses in quiet positions off the beaten track.

VILLAGES OR HAMLETS WITH GENERAL STORES

Kemble, Crudwell, Tetbury, Long Newnton, Malmesbury, Sherston, Grittleton, Castle Combe, Batheaston, Bathford, Bathampton.

TOURIST INFORMATION OFFICES

Cheltenham, Cirencester, Tetbury, Malmesbury, Bradford-on-Avon, Bath.

3

THE CORNISH PATH

he wild Atlantic lashing the forbidding cliffs and booming into secret caves hidden from the walker's gaze; slate houses standing four-square to the wind; the scattered relics of the abandoned tin mines; the eternal cry of the seagulls – this is the stuff of the Cornish path. Inland, the county is less spectacular: our route crosses the narrow Penwith isthmus through little wooded valleys and across wind-swept heaths. Stately old farmhouses shelter beneath ancient stands of beech in a landscape that is littered with Celtic field boundaries and ancient monuments. In the ever-mild woods and gardens flourish fuchsia, veronica, hydrangea and spring anemone.

Cornish geology is straightforward: several granite intrusions (Bodmin Moor, St Austell, Redruth, Penwith and the Scilly Isles) burst up through the Devonian slate which varies across the county from bluish-silver to deep green. Our path keeps to the slaty matrix, skirting the granite outcrops and avoiding the colourful serpentine in the Lizard peninsula.

The historical reasons for selecting this route are explained later. The Cornish path shares with one of the walks across the island of Mull the wildest landscapes in the book. Here we choose to link the old villages and settlements along the way by using the long-distance footpath along the north Cornish coast for almost the whole distance. In fact, walkers who have explored the whole of Cornwall's coastline often consider this bracing Atlantic stretch to be the most magnificent of all. When the sun shines the sea turns peacock blue, and the sight of Godrevy lighthouse standing four-square to this background while the Trinity House helicopter flew in with supplies has proved unforgettable.

No English county except Wiltshire is as rich in prehistoric remains as Cornwall. The county abounds in ancient barrow tombs and cromlechs – the stone burial chambers that remain when the

earth mounds are eroded away. The prosperity of Cornwall rested on tin, which was mined in many places and traded as far as the Phoenician territory in modern Lebanon. The Romans, too, exploited the tin, but nothing else, so Roman remains are almost non-existent.

In 815 Egbert, the Saxon king of Wessex, subdued a Celtic civilisation of great spiritual power. He would have found much evidence of these saintly Celts: the tiny stone cells of Celtic monks are among the oldest Christian buildings in England. There are twenty-five inscribed stones dating from the fourth to the tenth centuries, and over three hundred stone crosses in churchyards, churches, along roads and in private gardens. Saxon place-names occur in the east of the county, but Celtic names predominate in the west. King Aethelstan established a see at St Germans, still the most ambitious medieval church in Cornwall, while Tintagel gives the best idea of a Norman parish church: cruciform, unaisled and with a tower over the crossing.

The Life and Cult of St Piran

St Piran was supposedly sent from Ireland to England as a missionary by St Patrick. A tall and powerful figure, Piran became the patron saint of Cornwall – his banner, a white cross on a black ground, is allegedly the old standard of Dumnonia, as the Celtic kingdom was called, and symbolised the gospel triumphant over falsehood. St Piran's feast is commemorated on 5 March, especially at Perranzabuloe.

After Piran's death in about 580, his relics were venerated by pilgrims, and many thousands benefited from his holy aura by interment close to his remains. As the moving sands churned up the graveyard around the little oratory, so many fragments of their brittle bones came to the surface that, according to observers in 1835, the surrounding sand turned almost white.

St Piran came to be canonised because in the Church at this date the title of saint was conferred posthumously on the founder of a church, chapel or religious community – hence the great number of Cornish and Breton tutelary saints. From about the tenth century onwards, formal canonisation in the Roman Church depended upon proof of unusual piety.

The historian Canon Gilbert Doble wrote in *The Saints of Cornwall* (1965):

We have more information as to the cult paid to St Perran at Perranzabuloe before the Reformation than about the cult of any other Cornish saint, and, standing at the lonely oratory amid the sand hills or the great stone cross close by, we feel, more than anywhere else in the country, that we are treading in the footsteps of one of the makers of Christian Cornwall . . . Everywhere in Cornwall we find the names of Celtic saints who founded our churches, but here we see, undisturbed by later associations of Gothic churches or modern houses, the spot where one of them lived, still to some extent as it was in his time and in the ages which immediately followed.

The striking hexagonal tower of Godrevy Lighthouse marks the east end of St Ives Bay, point of entry for prehistoric gold and the Celtic saints from Ireland

We can see the extent of Piran's teaching or popularity in ancient Dumnonia in the churches dedicated to St Piran: three Cornish parishes at Perranzabuloe or Perran in the Sands; Perranuthnoe, or Perran the Little, near Marazion; and Perranarworthal on the north end of Falmouth Harbour, as well as the chapel at Trethevy in the parish of Tintagel. Two dedications in Brittany, at Trézélidé and St Perran, probably reflect the saint's travels.

The Lonely Oratory on Penhale Sands

All around St Piran's Oratory roll 40ft (12m) high dunes which are well covered with marram grass, although this does not prevent them from moving slowly. The cycle of the revelation of the oratory suggests that the ruins were partially visible in the eighteenth century, but by Regency times they were again lost to view. In about 1890 the site was revealed or discovered and subsequently excavated. By 1910 the site had become so threatened

ZENNOR HEAD

GURNARD'S
HEAD

ST IVE'S HEAD

GODREVY POINT

ST IVES

HELL'S MOUTH

CARBIS BAY

PH GWITHIAN

TREVARNON
ROUND

PHILLACK

LELANT

A30

HAYLE COPPERHOUSE

PH

CAN

MADRON

CROWLAS

ST ERTH

TREWINNARD MANOR

PH

SETTLEMENT

A30

PENZANCE

TRUTHWALL

GWALLON

NEWLYN

MARAZION

PRIORY

GOLDSITHNEY

ST MICHAEL'S MOUNT

PERRANUTHNOE

MOUSEHOLE

GERMOE

CUDDEN
POINT

CASTLE

HOE POINT

CELTIC CROSS AT PHILLACK CHURCH

ORNISH PATH

TOWAN POINT

KELSEY HEAD

PENHALE POINT

LIGGER POINT

PERRAN BEACH

St PIRAN'S CELL

A3075

CLIGGA HEAD

St AGNES' HEAD

B3285

† PERRANPORTH

TUBBY'S HEAD
WHEAL COATES

St AGNES
BEACON

† St AGNES

CHAPEL PORTH

PERRANZABULOE

B3285

PORTHTOWAN

† PORTREATH

NE CASTLE

† † REDRUTH

CELTIC CROSS AT
GWITHIAN CHURCH

KILOMETRES
MILES

St PIRAN'S CROSS AND BANNER

by the moving sands that a concrete 'bus garage' was built over the top. In 1980 the Department of the Environment gave up trying to keep even the garage accessible. Now the oratory and its shelter lie below the sand once again, marked by a rough granite plinth.

A good track leads from the metalled road (SW 775553) through gorse and then onto the rolling heath, where the path for the ruins is marked by small square limestone blocks every 44-110yd (40-100m). If you get lost, head for a tall wooden cross on a high dune: the oratory lies about 220yd (200m) north of it. The second church is then visible, close to a stone Celtic cross 656yd (600m) to the east. In winter it is a very lonely place with skylarks your only companions, and even in summer the rolling dunes would hide someone quite close to hand.

Although the Celtic ruin is called an 'oratory' this description is inaccurate – far from being a cell for a single monk, excavations revealed that it was used for services by many people. So it should properly be called a chapel, or, since it once contained relics of the saint, a shrine.

Edwardian excavators of St Piran's Oratory found substantial remains standing, right to the height of one gable end, with a window and a door ornamented with three carved heads. Inside a stone bench ran around the walls. Although very difficult to date, modern opinion ascribes this chapel to the eighth century, but it was probably built on the site of Piran's actual oratory.

As early as the eleventh century the little community gave up the struggle against the encroaching sand and water, and built themselves a bigger chapel, which later became the parish church, on the higher dune close to the limit of sanctuary marked by the tenth-century cross. These ruins are still accessible.

Fragments revealed from time to time and comparison with more complete Celtic monasteries in Ireland indicate that we should imagine a modest settlement around the church. Unlike the magnificent later medieval monasteries, these Celtic communities consisted of many small and separate buildings: refectory, guest-house, individual monks' cells, school, barn and abbot's cell. There

are suggestions, too, of an anchorite's cell, a holy well and a mill on the stream through the site.

The lovely cross is undoubtedly the most evocative survival of the early shrine. One of the best preserved in Cornwall, it stands about 8ft (2.4m) above the rough grass and is called 'Christes-mace' in a charter of 960. Four holes pierce the wheelhead, but only three penetrate right through. Like the cross we shall see at Phillack, it marked the boundary and entrance to the *llan*, or sacred enclosure.

The monastery formed the centre of the manor of Lanpiran. Its houses may have been near the monastery as well. Gradually, however, the settlement moved to firmer ground inland, so that in 1804 the parishioners rebuilt the church in a more convenient spot.

· THE CORNISH PATH DESCRIBED ·

From Penhale Sands to Perranzabuloe
Standing at St Piran's Oratory the whole of the seaward side is Ministry of Defence property, connecting with Penhale Camp to the north. There is, however, a right of way along the footpath marked on the OS map from the oratory on a bearing of 260° – though in these tall and ever-shifting dunes a straight footpath is a mere figment of a cartographer's imagination; the rule is to go west as far as the coast, then turn south along the top of the storm beach.

The first feature is Gear Sands holiday camp, which is built on slightly firmer ground a little way back from the sea. Although this group of chalets above the dunes is totally deserted in the winter, the summer antics of holidaymakers on the beach must make a strange contrast with walkers on the coastal path.

At the end of Perran Beach we pass behind the rocks at Cotty's Point and around the cove of the pretty village of Perranporth, the last place for some miles where walkers will encounter all the facilities they might need. At this point there is a choice of route: you can either carry straight on and tackle the finest stretch of the Cornish Coast Long Distance Path, or make a historical detour inland to find out what happened to the church of St Piran.

One of the finest early Christian crosses in Cornwall still rises above the dunes to mark the eastern boundary of St Piran's Celtic monastery (Photo: author)

St Piran on Firmer Ground

The detour entails a 2 mile (3km) walk to the settlement called Lambourne (SW 770520) via a winding lane and a disused railway line. The goal is to visit the very pretty third church of St Piran at Perranzabuloe, known formerly as Perran in Sabulo – that is, 'in the sands', although its new site is miles from the dunes. What happened is that the name of the second church on Penhale Sands remained when the parishioners finally gave up their centuries-old battle with the dunes and moved to the site of their new homes in 1804. They brought with them many historic fragments, monuments, furnishings and, of course, the church plate. The building was medievalised in 1879 and many exotic trees were planted in the churchyard during the nineteenth century, so that the whole picturesque scene is well worth seeing, if only for the contrast with the barren ruins of its two predecessors. The verger here has made an accurate model of St Piran's Oratory, now kept in the south transept, which shows better than any words what the original Celtic shrine looked like.

The Cornish Coastal Path

Our main path continues on the long-distance path (marked 'LDP' on the Ordnance Survey) from here to the port of Hayle. A native Cornishman who has walked the whole of the coastal path maintains that this is the best part of the Cornwall coast for walkers, even if they do head into the prevailing westerlies. The National Trust has acquired a good proportion of this coast for preservation through their Enterprise Neptune appeal, especially the mining site called Wheal Coates (SW 701500) and the long stretch from Portreath to Godrevy Towans.

No walker will need any encouragement to admire the drama and rugged beauty of these coves and headlands that stand high above the fury of the open Atlantic. Almost every museum in Cornwall seems to glory in the huge number of shipwrecks along this treacherous coastline. Cornwall is noted for its lack of standing timber, but with such quantities of ships' timbers cast up by history onto the foreshore, one imagines that the builders of old had no worries over a shortage of roof-beams. No directions are needed to follow the coastal path: the route would be obvious in our section even if it were not so well marked by the Countryside Commission, for it never leaves the coast all the way to Hayle.

After rounding Cligga Head, Bawden Rocks come into view about a mile out to sea and form a splendid feature. The first detour around the head of a deep gully occurs at Trevaunance Cove. Just inland, above the steep slopes of the coombe, intact ritual deposits were found when Trevellas round barrow was excavated in 1940. (The 'Tre' prefix is the commonest element in Cornish place-names; it simply means a farm.)

Steep Streets at St Agnes

If you found the village of Perranporth slightly spoiled by its facilities for the holiday campers, St Agnes will be more to your taste. The absence of a sandy beach within easy walking distance has spared St Agnes, a remarkably unspoilt stone village on a steep site. All kinds of refreshment are to be found – for example, fresh and genuine Cornish pasties are sold next to the church. Anyone with a magpie instinct will head for the Railway Inn with its amazing collections of shoes, naval memorabilia and brasses.

A reconstruction of the chapel at St Agnes' Well on the Cornish coast

The parish church of St Agnes occupies a very steep curving site, that was cunningly exploited by the architect Piers St Aubyn in 1848 when he rebuilt it in the Cornish tradition.

Local heroes include the famous Cornish portrait painter John Opie (1761-1807) who was born near St Agnes and the successful journalist John Passmore Edwards (1823-1911), founder of numerous public libraries and museums.

St Agnes Beacon to Portreath

In clear weather, and especially just after a rainstorm has washed the dust out of the atmosphere, it is worth continuing from the village via St Agnes Beacon (628ft/192m/SW 710503) where the view encompasses most of Cornwall, including our objective, St Michael's Mount. Closer to hand extends the typical north Cornwall landscape; short-turfed, undulating, wind-swept, treeless and speared by the chimneys of old tin mines. Three unexcavated cairns on the summit of St Agnes Beacon could be burials, or just mining heaps. From there a footpath rejoins the coast north of Tubby's Head. In low cloud it would be preferable to keep to the coastal path around St Agnes Head.

After passing Tubby's Head you will see what the Royal Commission on Historical Monuments describes officially as 'an alleged stone circle' (SW 700508). Megalithic monument or not, it consists of a group of twelve boulders about 18in (46cm) high arranged in a rough circle 24-30ft (7-9m) across. Its irregular shape should not count against its antiquity, for most genuine stone 'circles' are not circular at all, but describe complex geometrical figures.

No visit to Cornwall would be complete without a trip to a tin mine. Fortunately, the coastal path soon reaches a mine that is so well preserved and spectacularly sited that it forms an epitome of the

Cornish landscape. The National Trust maintains at Wheal Coates (SW 701500) two mine buildings, one above the cliffs and the other some way down towards the crashing surf.

At the next little cove, Chapel Porth, are remains closer to our theme. On the north-east side of the narrow defile, look for a level platform. This is the site of the medieval St Agnes Well and chapel. Although the chapel was destroyed in 1780 and the small building which covered the sacred spring similarly collapsed in about 1820, a welling of water may still be seen. All that remains on the platform is a turf-covered wall footing oriented south-west to north-east and measuring 39 × 23ft (12 × 7m).

Should you twist your ankle or want to alert the coastguard on this long stretch of lonely coast, there is a telephone box at the end of the track leading down the coombe into Chapel Porth. The next cove, Porthtowan (meaning the harbour in the dunes), has a pub, a post office and a shop. But the next proper village which is full of facilities is Portreath (about 7 miles (11km) along the path from St Agnes), a rather drab place in the bay beyond the disused aerodrome on Nancekuke Common. Nikolaus Pevsner must have felt the same when, in his *Buildings of England: Cornwall,* he described the early Victorian church of St Mary's, Portreath, as 'rather depressing'.

Past Hell's Mouth

From here around to the lighthouse at Godrevy Point the coastal scenery becomes, if anything, even more magnificent. Once again public contributions to the National Trust's Enterprise Neptune fund have ensured that it stays that way. After the first two minor headlands the path reaches an Iron Age promontory fort called Crane Castle (SW 634440). This cliff-top fort is defended on the landward side by double ramparts 262ft (80m) long and about 7½ft (2.3m) high. There is no trace of an entrance and the ends of the ramparts are slowly disappearing into the sea as a result of erosion. 'Crane' is probably a corruption of Kerhen, meaning 'old or abandoned fort'. The view from here of Basset's Cove and Crane Islands far below is immensely impressive.

Associated with this fort are six barrows on Reskajeage Downs, but these tombs have all been ploughed out and nothing can be seen, except from the air. After Deadman's Cove (and how many sailors, one wonders, met their deaths on these rocks?) the path reaches another barrow which can be made out, 23ft (7m) in diameter and 3ft (1m) high, but cut in half by coastal erosion. Look for it on the east side of tiny Hudder Cove (SW 607431). If there is any swell running at all, attention is likely to be distracted from the Iron Age remains hereabouts by a deep booming sound, as the waves crash into the famous cleft in the rocks here known as Hell's Mouth, accompanied only by the ceaseless screaming of the seagulls.

St Ives Bay

Rounding Godrevy Point we see the last of the Atlantic cliffs, but in leaving them we reach perhaps the most delightful feature of all along the north Cornish coast. Seen from the low slaty foreshore, no tower could look lovelier than Godrevy lighthouse. Its tapering hexagonal shape, brilliantly white against the blue sea, is a most striking piece of sculpture in an exceptionally fine setting. Prominent on the headland is another round barrow.

Here we are back in the dunes, and, like Penhale Sands, they also conceal an ancient oratory. According to the Cornish church-visitors' vade-mecum:

> Gwithian has long been a chapelry to Phillack, but in the twelfth century it seems to have been a distinct *ecclesia*. In the sandy waste between the village and the sea there was, by tradition, a city of *Connor*. This is perhaps derived from the Irish *Conair* (a haven). A highly interesting oratory of the Celtic period lies beneath the sand. It was excavated in the last century but has since become buried. It is more perfect than the oratory of St Piran, having been less meddled with, though it is probably not so ancient.
>
> *The Cornish Church Guide* (1925) Anon

Gwithian oratory dates from 900 to 950 and is considered to be the successor of a Celtic shrine on the same spot. A graveyard lay to the south and

Towanroath engine house, an evocative relic of the Cornish tin mining industry preserved near Chapel Porth

east of it, but the encroaching sands of Gwithian Towans caused it, like its sister oratory of St Piran, to be abandoned: the parishioners built a new church on firmer ground in the thirteenth century.

The new St Gwithian, or Gocianus, stands in a pretty churchyard with a quiet pub beside it – such proximity is usually a result of the old tradition of 'church ales'. Supposedly the parish stored ale for celebrating its holy days in a convenient cellar near the consecrated ground, the ale store at some time being turned into a pub. The present church was rebuilt on its medieval foundations in 1866 by the architect E. Sedding senior who incorporated old fragments, such as the lychgate, the entire tower and the chancel arch. The result is attractive and, like St Agnes, typically Cornish. It was for long a chapelry to Phillack, the next parish on our route,

and its curious medieval privileges, for instance wreck rights, may be vestiges of a small Celtic principality here. On the south side of the churchyard stands an old cross, 4ft 8in (1.5m) high with a beaded rim, which was probably erected in the twelfth century to mark the consecration of the graveyard.

About 2/3 mile (1km) south of Gwithian church is an extensive earthwork called Trevarnon Round (SW 587402), which is accessible by a footpath from either road. It has a moat and rampart, and, like the round at St Erth, probably dates from the Iron Age. Judging simply from the site, its function must have been agricultural rather than defensive.

From Gwithian follow the coastal path along the dunes as far as SW 562393 and make a choice: either continue around the headland to Black Cliff and get a good view of the unusually safe landing-place afforded by the sandy beaches of St Ives' Bay, or turn south-east on the footpath to the important old settlement at Phillack.

The Safe Haven in Hayle Estuary

Hayle was immensely important in both pre-historic and early Christian times because of the safe anchorage in its estuary. Not only is it the only natural harbour on the north Cornish coast, but if the skipper's navigation is askew or the winds unfavourable, the ship will end up safely on the gently shelving beach on either side of the river mouth. These essential advantages made it the point of entry for Irish gold and copper as far back as the Bronze Age, and of Christian missionaries in those centuries when Ireland, Wales, Cornwall and Brittany formed a tightly knit Celtic world.

Although Phillack is now a quiet hamlet on the way to nowhere, it was a most important place during Celtic times, the years before 930 and English domination. Between 500 and 550 a wave of Irish missionaries came to west Cornwall through Hayle. Among them was St Piala, whose name became corrupted into Phillack. In Phillack's churchyard we can cast aside the mass of speculative literature which has arisen around the Irish evangelists and listen instead to the contemporary carvings.

High in the gable of the south porch is the 'Chi-Rho stone' (the first two letters of Christos), dated on stylistic grounds to 350-450, and presumably once forming a part of the first Celtic church. So Phillack church might even pre-date the mission of St Piala. The lychgate incorporates a much-worn relief carving of the crucifixion in which Christ wears a long Byzantine tunic, supposedly influenced by trade contacts before 650 between western Britain and the eastern Mediterranean. Such crosses appear in Ireland and Wales until the ninth century. There is also a tall tenth-century churchyard cross, depicting the crucifixion in a Celtic wheelhead. The sharp relief of the carving remains on the lower shaft of the cross because it was protected by the graves which rose around it for centuries, until the Victorians dug it up and re-stored it to its original height.

Phillack's parish church has a long and elaborate history. It once drew tithes from nearly 3,000 acres (1,214ha) along the coast, including what is today the parish of Gwithian. A little Norman work can be found in the building, but the tower and some woodwork are fifteenth century, while the rest is a rebuilding of 1856 by the eccentric architect William White. The churchyard is now large, but the bank closer to the church and the steep drop to the road indicate the Celtic boundary.

Hayle has all the facilities of a small town, but very little of scenic value except the railway viaduct, the old mill at Copperhouse* and the view of the saltings from the ambience of the pub called the Old Quay House at Griggs Quay (SW 545363). The local heroine is Elizabeth Arden who was born at Hayle in 1884, while the local hero is now the entrepreneur Peter de Savary who intends to re-vitalise the town's economy by developing the tourist potential of the tawdry harbour.

Across the Isthmus of Penwith
The path leaves the coast at Hayle to cross the narrow 3¾ mile (6km) isthmus that divides Penwith from the rest of Cornwall. The best route for walkers passes through the attractive village of

*Hayle Copperhouse: in a field a few yards from the the road at the top of Steamer Hill is the engine house of the first steam-using railway in Cornwall, which was built in 1834 to carry ore from the mines near Hayle to smelting works at Redruth.

St Erth. The first mile is along a lane under the main A30 and runs close to the right bank of the little River Hayle. Erth is a corruption of the Celtic name Rrygh or Herygh. Here there is a late medieval market cross, a lovely square and a fourteenth-century bridge which once formed the head of navigation on the river. Here the local hero is one of the most famous Cornishmen of all, Richard Trevithick, the inventor and railway pioneer, who was married to Jane Harvey at St Erth church in 1797.

The most memorable feature of St Erth is the exquisite churchyard, which is full of beautiful trees, shrubs and flowers, as well as curious monuments and two ancient sculptures – a Celtic cross head and a granite cross found on a nearby farm. The church, like Phillack's, is an early foundation. Extensive eighteenth- and nineteenth-century re-buildings have left only the tower and some of the nave pillars from the Middle Ages. Look for a grotesque head on the tower below the battlements. The interior of the church is graced by a traditional Cornish waggon roof in the porch, and an elaborate roof and screen in the Edwardian Lady Chapel. Above the vicarage is another Iron Age round, enclosing 2 acres (0.8ha) inside a double rampart.

We can now pick up a farm track on the other, or left, bank of the River Hayle as far as a livery stable/cattery/farm. Then a rather muddy footpath leads off to the right past Trewinnard Manor, a rough but splendid Stuart farm with a shell porch and the foundations of a fourteenth-century chapel on the front lawn. The footpath continues on to Tregetlias Farm, then to Tregilliowe Farm, and finally to the hamlet of Truthwall, where there is a small medieval hall house. This place commands our first view of the English Channel.

After the attractive hamlet of Gwallon, the route passes underneath the main A394 road (at SW 524317) and follows a footpath to Home Farm (SW 520319). A lane contours around the hill on the left bank of the Red River and finally crosses it on a beautiful old bridge, which has the unusual feature of a free-standing milestone in one of the breakwaters. This route gives the best approach to St Michael's Mount, which now appears as we re-

Bassett's Cove and the rampart of Crane Castle – half the fort has already fallen down the cliff into the Atlantic

join the coastal path for the final stretch into the village of Marazion.

Marazion does not, as has been absurdly asserted, derive its name from 'the Bitter Waters of Zion', but is a corruption of Market Jew or Jeudi, that is, Thursday Market. The Cutty Sark in Marazion Square is the preferred watering hole and lodging.

The Cult of St Michael
Who knows not St Michael's Mount and chair,
The Pilgrims' Holy Vaunt?
Both land and island twice a day,
Both fort and port of haunt.
Richard Carew (1602)

Despite its remoteness, Cornwall had its fair share of popular medieval pilgrimages. There was, for example, the shrine known as the 'Holy Trinity of St Day' at Gwennap, a parish near Redruth, where the fifteenth-century church was so thoroughly stripped and refurnished by the Victorians that absolutely nothing remains to tell the modern visitor of the faithful who once flocked there.

Only slightly less popular was St Piran's Cell, followed by St Germans, a little medieval town on the safe anchorage afforded by the River Lynher in the south-east of the county. Here the evidence is more than literary, for St Germans' church is the finest of Cornwall's Norman buildings. The only other local saint with the reputation of attracting the faithful from east of the Tamar estuary was St Petroc, whose shrine was at Bodmin.

St Michael's Mount
More popular than any of these five places was St Michael's Mount. It seems likely, although it cannot be proved, that the sanctity of the island during the Middle Ages owes something to its pagan past. Even today it is not difficult to sense the sheer magic of the place, especially during the

winter when there are few people to be seen. We may imagine prehistoric men making the journey to the lustrous island off the rocky coast, as they did to the mystical Isle of Avalon.

Prehistoric traders used the island as a port from very early times and by the Iron Age it had become highly important for the continental export trade in gold and copper from Ireland and tin from Cornwall. Traders believed that it was much safer to bring goods into the estuary at Hayle on the north coast and make an easy 3 mile (5km) journey across the narrow and level isthmus than to risk sailing around the dangerous peninsula of Land's End. There was certainly a settlement here during the Iron Age – it is one of the few places in Britain to which Mediterranean traders had given a name, Ictis Insula, before Julius Caesar's raids. Pytheas, a geographer from the Greek colony of Marseilles, had explored the coast of Britain during the fourth century BC and we know of his findings from the later account of Diodorus:

> The inhabitants of that part of Britain which is called Belerion are very fond of strangers and from their intercourse with foreign merchants are civilised in their manner of life. They prepare the tin, working very carefully the earth in which it is produced. The ground is rocky but contains earthy veins, whose produce is ground down, smelted and purified. They beat the metal into masses shaped like knuckle-bones and carry it to a certain island off Britain called Ictis. During the ebb of the tide the intervening space is left dry and they carry over to the island the tin in abundance in their wagons . . . Here the merchants buy the tin and carry it over to Gaul, and after travelling overland for about thirty days, they finally bring their loads on mules to the mouth of the Rhône.

The traders were probably Veneti from Brittany who used sound oak ships with high prows and leather sails.

There is little archaeological evidence to confirm the prehistoric tin trade. At Marazion an ancient smelting pit and portions of a bronze cauldron came to light in the last century, while bronze battle axes, swords and spear-heads were found at the foot of the mount several hundred years before,

according to the historian Camden.

A puzzling fact is that the old Cornish name for St Michael's Mount meant 'the grey rock in the forest', while William of Worcester visited the place in 1478 and found that it had been called 'the hore-rock in the wood'. Does this mean that the identification of the island with the ancient Ictis is wrong? The answer is 'probably not', because this forest can be explained by the remains of ancient tree-trunks that were discovered in Mount's Bay, dated by the Natural History Museum to at least 2000BC.

The Archangel Michael

Of the mount's prehistoric religious significance we know nothing except what we can infer from its legendary connection with St Michael. According to an old Cornish legend, the Archangel Michael appeared to some fishermen in 495, standing high above them on a ledge of rock at the west side of the island.

The Archangel Michael is one of the Christian saints who appears in the Old Testament. His name means 'Who is like unto God' and the Book of Daniel presents him as 'one of the chief princes' of the heavenly host and as the special protector of Israel. In the New Testament's Book of Revelation he is the principal soldier in the heavenly battle against the devil who appears in the form of a dragon. His formal cult probably began in the East under the Emperor Constantine who built a church in St Michael's honour at Sosthenion near Constantinople.

From early times St Michael's cult has been strong in the British Isles where many prominent places are associated with his name, one of the most spectacular being the Great Skellig, or Skellig Michael, a monstrous rock in the open Atlantic off the coast of County Kerry. The significance of the prominent summits may be that they are closer to the heavenly scene of the conflict between Michael and the devil. Whatever the exact connection, there are certainly numerous hilltop churches dedicated to the Archangel Michael all over Britain.

William of Worcester records in his *Itinerarium* that St Michael appeared on the summit of the Cornish mount in about 710, as he had previously done at the Italian sanctuary of Monte San Galgano.

In honour of this vision the Celtic Church founded a monastery on the mount soon afterwards, although little of its history is known until the saintly Edward the Confessor gave it during the 1040s to the abbey of Mont-Saint-Michel in Normandy to become a dependent cell of Benedictine monks. So began the association between St Michael's two mystical islands on either side of the English Channel.

The Connection with Mont-Saint-Michel

Mont-Saint-Michel is a larger version of the Cornish mount, but is also joined to the mainland by a causeway which is cut twice a day by the tide. The island rises from a small bay in Normandy. Its importance dates from 708, when the Archangel Michael appeared three times in a vision to the Bishop of Avranches, who later became St Aubert. Following his heavenly instructions he built a sanctuary on the summit which became a wealthy Benedictine abbey under the direct patronage of the powerful dukes of Normandy.

Unless the relevant charter was a forgery, the abbey was given the Cornish mount in the mid-eleventh century, but successive abbots took no steps to develop their dependent cell until 1135. The little priory on St Michael's Mount took nine years to build and, when finished, housed a religious community of a prior and twelve monks. Each year one of them had to visit Mont-Saint-Michel and pay a tribute of sixteen marks. Furthermore, each new brother had to cross the Channel and receive the abbot's blessing. In 1155 Hadrian IV, the only English pope, confirmed all the English possessions of Mont-Saint-Michel, including St Michael's Mount.

The priory prospered as it had a good income from fairs, markets and watermills, as well as receiving tithes of fish and timber. During the long wars with France, the English kings were angered by the priory's allegiance and financial assistance to the enemy. Frequently they seized the priory's revenues, only granting them to Mont-Saint-Michel during intervals of peace. Eventually, Henry V appropriated the priory as alien property and granted it as an endowment to the Brigittine Abbey of Syon near London.

The Pilgrimage

As pilgrimage became more and more common in the high Middle Ages, the shrine of the Archangel Michael was the most popular and famous in the West of England, boasting miraculous cures, several relics and a papal indulgence, as well as a healthy income – £7 in 1431 – from the gifts of the faithful.

The story of a miraculous cure in 1262 was discovered in a manuscript kept at Avranches, near Mont-Saint-Michel:

> Let no-one going to the monastery of St Michael in Cornwall doubt that a certain woman named Christina, of the neighbourhood of Glastonbury, who had been deprived of the sight of her eyes for about six years, coming with the greatest devotion to the said monastery for the sake of prayer and pilgrimage, on the 14th May 1262, before High Mass on a certain Sunday, in the sight of the people, persevering in the greatest faith, by intercession of the Blessed Archangel Michael, recovered miraculously the sight of her closed eyes. There were present as witnesses many monks and others.

We know of several relics that were kept at the shrine to attract pilgrims in the Middle Ages. Like relics all over England and Wales, they were either broken up or sold for their gold and jewels to swell the royal coffers at the dissolution of the monasteries. One of the most important relics was the jawbone of St Apollonia, who was martyred at Alexandria by the slow extraction of all her teeth, after which she was burned alive. She became the patron saint of dentists and to this day appears in this role as a supporter of the arms of the British Dental Association.

From an inventory made in 1430 for the Abbess of Syon we know the lay-out and contents of St Michael's church. The famous sculpture of the Archangel Michael slaying the dragon (that is, the devil) with a lance stood near the entrance – an image of this appears on the map. Flanking the high altar were the altars of St Michael and the crucified Saviour. Among the relics kept in an elaborate box on the high altar were 'a part of the Holy Cross enclosed in silver' and Henry VI's

sword and spurs, which were venerated because of their owner's piety.

Rituals at St Michael's Mount

The mystical island of St Michael's Mount, or Ictis, *seen here cut off from the Cornish mainland by high tide*

The rituals associated with the pilgrimage to this shrine are peculiar and unique, and it is not difficult to visualise them in the very places around the mount where they occurred. Pilgrims would await the fall of the tide at Chapel Rock near the Marazion end of the causeway. The chapel there was dedicated to the Virgin Mary and was demolished during the Civil Wars in 1645, when parliamentary forces laid siege to the castle.

Following a decree by the abbot, pilgrims would perform a penance as they walked across to the island by placing one stone in the causeway. Then half-way over to the mount they would offer a prayer at the pilgrim cross, whose socket may still be seen in a rock on the left. The original cross has now been removed to the gardens just below the castle and there is also a replica outside the church door.

After the donation of alms and the veneration of the relics in the shrine, the pilgrims took part in a strange ritual involving a feat of bravado which illustrates the bizarre sense of humour of medieval man. As an act of faith, a pilgrim would climb out onto the notorious St Michael's chair, which was suspended above an awesome drop down to the raging sea some 250ft (76m) below. Richard Carew described it in 1602 as a 'bad seat and craggy place called St Michael's chair somewhat dangerous for access and therefore holy for the adventure'. Islanders believed that the windier it was, the more valuable was the ordeal to the pilgrim's soul. This is not difficult to believe, for the stone chair projected from the parapet of the church tower where the beacon now rises. The chair is no longer available for modern pilgrims to demonstrate their faith. The origin of this strange custom is obscure. Could it have been some re-enactment of the temptation of Christ in the wilderness, when the devil invited Jesus to cast himself from a precipice?

St Michael's Mount Today

The long and interesting military history of St Michael's Mount stretches back to the time of the Crusades. During the Civil Wars, parliamentary forces, after capturing the castle in 1646, installed as constable Colonel John St Aubyn. He so liked the place that he bought the whole island. The St Aubyn family have lived on St Michael's Mount ever since, gradually converting a medieval fortress into a comfortable mansion.

The public tour of the castle includes all the principal rooms of the mansion. The priory church itself remains in regular use for public worship. It stands, naturally, on the very summit of the granite rock. Most of the structure is fourteenth century, with a beautiful rose window at either end from a

Aerial view of St Michael's Mount showing the medieval priory. Pilgrims climbed into the chair on the tower. The foreground ship is taken from a stained-glass window in the former monks' refectory

hundred years later. The St Aubyn family pews are on either side of the chancel.

The Lady Chapel to the north-east of the church is a lovely building which hangs prominently overhead on the way up from the harbour. The family converted it during the reign of George II into the 'Blue Drawing-room', whose delicate rococo interior and jaunty Gothic plasterwork make an astonishing contrast to the austere and grim rooms inside the castle itself.

The remainder of the monastic buildings were destroyed during remodelling in the eighteenth century, with the single exception of the monks' refectory, or dining hall. Now called the Chevy Chase Room, only the walls and a few of the roof timbers are original.

The architect Piers St Aubyn, a cousin of the then owner, skilfully extended the castle between 1873 and 1878 with a Victorian wing five floors deep – 'high' would be the wrong word, for during the public tour visitors stand level with the church on the roof of this suite. These rooms now form the private quarters of the 4th Lord St Levan. Great care was taken to prevent the Victorian wing from spoiling the island's famous silhouette.

The castle is open to the public every weekday during the summer, when there is a ferry service at high tide, and three days a week from November to May. Be warned, however, that the causeway can be closed for three days at a stretch during strong gales. On Sundays the public is welcome at the church service. Although his father vested the mount in the National Trust in 1954, the present Lord St Levan remains firmly in control of affairs on the island.

The castle gardens are a delight of romantic Victorian horticulture and the little orderly village by the harbour is charming. There was once a pub on the island, the St Aubyn Arms, but when the Prince of Wales, later Edward VII, paid a visit a retainer emerged from the bar and was less than respectful to the royal guest. Since that day the islanders have had to trek across to Marazion for alcoholic refreshment. Much to be recommended there is the Cutty Sark in the square, where the bedrooms are good value and some provide exquisite views of the mount.

THE CORNISH PATH:
ST PIRAN'S CELL TO ST MICHAEL'S MOUNT

ROUTE LENGTH: 31 miles (50km) · MAPS: OS 1:50,000 Nos 200, 203, 204

PUBLIC HOUSES

Map ref	Name of Pub	Location
SW 720505	Railway Inn***	Vicarage Road, St Agnes
		Collection of naval memorabilia
SW 744506	Miners Arms****#	Mithian, 1 mile (2km) S of path
SW 586413	Pendarves Arms*	Gwithian
SW 564384	Bucket of Blood**	Next to the church, Phillack
SW 545363	Old Quay House**	Griggs Quay, Hayle, ½ mile (1km) W of path
SW 517307	Cutty Sark**#	The Square, Marazion

Key: *** Highly recommended by the *Good Pub Guide*
    ** Recommended by the *Good Pub Guide*
     * Recommended
     # Accommodation

BED & BREAKFAST ACCOMMODATION

Map ref	Name of House	Location/Telephone number
SW 746506	Rose-in-the-Vale Hotel	Mithian. Tel: (087255) 2202,
		1 mile (2km) S of path
SW 520398	Old Vicarage	Parc-an-Creet, St Ives. Tel: (0736)796124,
		4 miles (7km) W of path

Both are historic buildings off the beaten track.

PUBLIC TELEPHONES

Map ref	Location of Telephone
SW 697494	Chapel Porth car park
SW 578413	Coastal path, St Peter's Point, near Gwithian

Pubs in each village and hamlet at reasonable hours.

VILLAGES OR HAMLETS WITH GENERAL STORES

Perranporth, St Agnes, Portreath, Phillack, Hayle, St Erth, Marazion.

TOURIST INFORMATION OFFICES

Newquay, Phillack (on the A30), St Ives.

4

THE ROAD TO THE ISLE

he pilgrimage to Iona is the most northerly route described in this book. Even among the many beautiful outposts in the Western Isles, Iona is a very special place – it was the spiritual capital which converted to Christianity the whole of Scotland and the large kingdom of Northumbria. For several centuries during the Dark Ages this Celtic monastery was one of the most important centres of European civilisation, keeping the Christian message alive at a time when pagans had triumphed almost everywhere in England.

The Life and Cult of St Columba

Columba was an Irish prince, born about AD521, who became a follower of St Patrick. His character might be considered unsaintly: his actions show that he was forceful, stubborn and ambitious. When a monk called Finian returned from Rome with a manuscript of the first Vulgate Gospels ever seen in Ireland, Columba was so covetous that he made an unauthorised copy for himself. Having been detected in his action, he resolutely refused to give up his copy, even when the High King of Ireland intervened against him in the growing dispute. Eventually, the trivial incident led to armed confrontation between his abbot's followers and those of Columba at the battle of Cul Dremne. Columba's supporters won the battle, but the Irish prince so regretted the enormous loss of life caused by his stubbornness that he vowed to leave Ireland and never to return.

So it happened that Columba sailed with twelve companions for the Western Isles, only stopping at Iona when he found that, from its summit, he could no longer see the Irish coast. The exiles found the island uninhabited and marked out the monastic

enclosure described below (pp72-4). But the restless Columba had little patience with a life of cloistered contemplation and was soon spreading the Christian message to the pagans of Mull and beyond into Argyll. There he converted the ruling house of Dalriada and pronounced Aidan its king in 574. Exploiting the similarity of the Irish and Pictish languages, he carried his mission all over Scotland, thereby spreading the gospel much further than St Ninian, St Kentigern, St Maolruabh and St Bride, who preached in their own areas.

Following Columba's death on Iona in 597, pilgrims came to venerate his relics in the cathedral. It is probable that the monks successfully hid the casket containing Columba's remains from marauding Vikings during their four early raids, and that his followers translated the true relics to Dunkeld, Perthshire, in 849 where they continued to attract pilgrims. The story that the marvellously waterproof reliquary floated miraculously to Downpatrick in County Down suggests intrigue and invention by the monks.

The Gospel Travels by Coracle from Iona

Strange as it may seem to us today when Iona seems so remote, in Columba's time the island proved an ideal centre for spreading the gospel, with missionaries going by sea, often in their tiny and fragile coracles, to all parts of Scotland and back to their roots in Ireland. In those early days Iona was a safe place to foster and disseminate learning, far from the barbarian strife in contemporary Europe.

The west door of St Columba's abbey, looking towards the Sound of Iona: the eighth-century St John's Cross was the model for many thousands of memorials from the 1890s

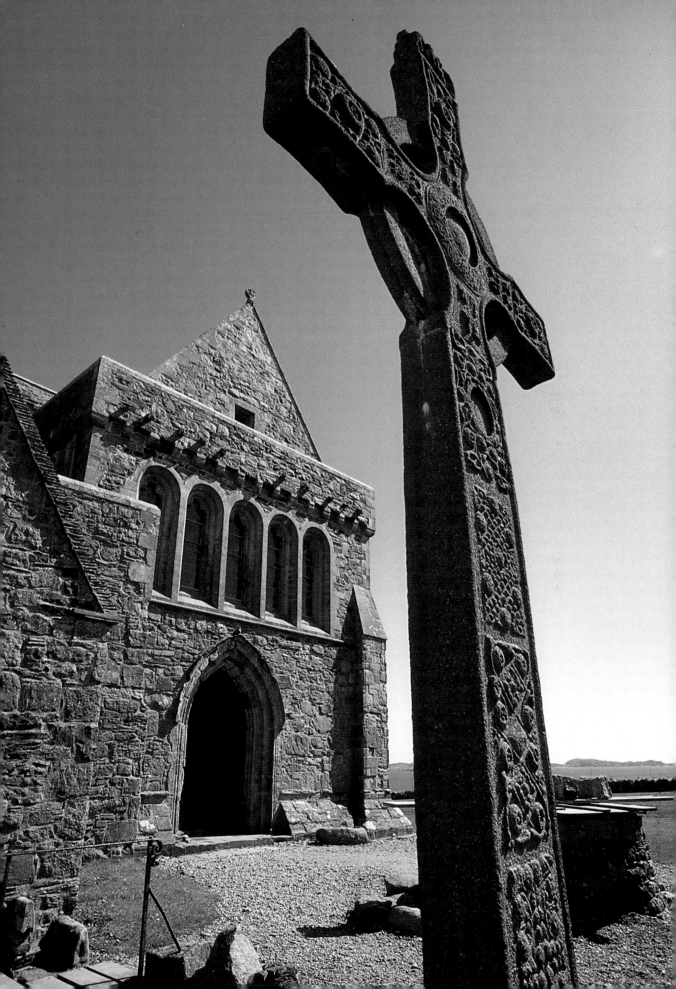

ST MARY'S CHAPEL
AND WELL

TOBERMORY

STANDING STONE

BURIAL GROUND

DERVAIG
STANDING STONES
STANDING STONES
SITE OF OLD CHAPEL
444m

BURIAL GROUND

TWO CLEARANCE
VILLAGE SITES
353m

KILNINIAN
CHURCH AND BURIAL GROUND
STANDING STANE

CHAPEL AND
BURIAL GROUN

LOCH TUATH

ULVA

CHAPEL

STAFFA
INCH KENNETH
CHAPEL

LOCH NA KEAL

BEN M

CHURCH

LOCH SCRIDAIN
CROSS

CROSSES
ABBEY
CROSSES

STANDING STONE

SITE OF OLD CHAPEL

FIONNPHORT
STANDING STONE
STANDING STONE
SITE OF OLD CHAPEL

BUNESSAN

IONA
NUN'S CAVE

KILOMETRES
MILES

CHURCH

CARSAIG ARCHES

ROAD TO THE ISLE

OBAN to IONA

ROS CASTLE

pennygown chapel

ardtornish castle

LISMORE

achadun castle

craignure

MULL

standing stone

duart castle

MODERN FERRY

dunollie castle

GRASS POINT

OBAN

ng stone

ne

church

KERRERA

BEN BUIE 717m

PORT NAM MARBH

gylen castle

stone circle
moy castle

ferry of the dead kings

chapel

LOCH FEOCHAN

SEIL

Disciples came from all parts in search of Columba's teaching, travelling across Mull by the 'Pilgrims' Way', which later became a drove road (see below). After his death in 597, Columba's reputation grew into a cult, attracting pilgrims right up to the dissolution of the monasteries in the sixteenth century. Columba's fame grew as a result of the enormous influence of Iona's missionaries, not just in the British Isles but throughout Christendom, for in the Dark Ages, when barbarians made travel so dangerous on the Continent, Celtic monks from Ireland and Iona were the bravest travellers in Europe, founding monasteries and spreading the word of God to such remote areas as the Apennines in northern Italy.

The Dead Return to Iona

As in life, so in death, the growing sanctity of Iona attracted the highest in the land to be brought far beyond their own country for burial in the Reilig Oran, or cemetery of the kings, next to the island's monastery. Here lie kings of Scotland, Ireland, Norway, the Isle of Man and Dalriada, as well as the romantic lords of the isles, clan chiefs, abbots and even, it is said, an archbishop of Canterbury. This astonishing tradition, lasting through ten centuries,* makes Iona unique: where else is it possible to find monarchs of four kingdoms, anxious to be remembered by their people, consenting to be taken for burial to such a remote island so far beyond their borders that few of their subjects would ever see their grave?

The unique sanctity of Iona as a royal burial ground has given this route a different character from all the other Christian pilgrimages in this book. Instead of seeking a shrine for the good of their own souls, pilgrims to Iona were part of the funeral cortège accompanying a king to his last resting place.

For those coming from the mainland, the cortège would embark with due ceremony from the shelter of Loch Feochan, south of modern Oban, and cross through Glen More and the Ross of Mull along the Pilgrims' Way. To the accompaniment of plucked

*Burials began on Iona in AD563 and continued until at least the end of the fifteenth century when the lordship of the isles was forfeited, while the Scottish kings were still brought to the island into the following century.

harps, another boat would slowly take the body across the Sound of Iona. Landing on the sands of Martyr's Bay, the cortège would then pass through the village and around the Nunnery along the 'Street of the Dead', whose ancient cobbled surface can now be seen again within the abbey precincts.

The Pilgrims' Way

The Pilgrims' Way begins either at Port nam Marbh (Harbour of the Dead) in south-east Mull, where funeral cortèges landed from Loch Feochan, or at nearby Grass Point, the former ferry terminal where cattle left for the mainland in the days before the Highland clearances banished both cattle and crofters from the island. The line of the Pilgrims' Way is still marked by five prehistoric standing stones (each Christianised by the incision of a cross), which may indicate that men have used this ancient trackway for four thousand years. A glance at the map will show that it is the easiest and safest way to travel from the mainland to Iona, the path reaching a height of only 670ft (205m) at the watershed in Glen More. Prehistoric or not, it was certainly a drovers' road in recent times.

Despite its historical importance, the Pilgrims' Way had become a secondary road by the time of World War II, when the ferry traffic went from Salen via Loch na Keal (Loch of the Cells of Missionaries) to Fionnphort and Iona. Now the old route has in part become the road from the new deep-water pier at Craignure to Iona; but walkers along the Pilgrims' Way who find a single-track road too busy can in many places still follow the ancient trackway where modern engineers have altered the line.

The Road from the 'Port of the Dead'

The scenic walk across Mull described below starts and ends at sensible places which are well served by ferries and buses. In tracing this historic route, however, we are including in this book the most remote beginning for a pilgrimage, for few people nowadays ever visit Port nam Marbh. In the Middle Ages the royal visitors may well have come here only after they were dead.

From among a series of possible landing places in south-east Mull it is unclear why Port nam

Marbh (NM 733278) came to be preferred. It was possible, for example, to sail right into Loch Don or Loch Spelve and save some of the land journey. But perhaps there was some long-forgotten ritual which could be performed only in this place.

A coastal path skirts around Carn Bàn (814ft/ 248m) to reach the old parish church of Killean (NM 710284). Today, the ruins stand only about 3ft (1m) high, but in 1393 the church received the honour of a papal indulgence that was granted in favour of pilgrims visiting it and making a donation. Possibly this special treatment resulted from its status as the first shrine on the funeral route.

A rough trackway across the turf leads north from near here to link up with the old drovers' road from Grass Point across the northern head of Loch Spelve. From here all the way to Fionnphort, the jetty for the Iona ferry, our historic route follows

Funeral cortège of a king of Dalriada crossing the Sound of Iona in about AD750

the single-track road. It would be tedious to walk all the way on the bitumen – nearly 31 miles (50km) – and many people might prefer to hitch a lift or bicycle. The gradients are now very easy for such a mountainous island. For the first half of the distance – that is, between the two sea lochs of Spelve and Scridain – you can walk for nearly all the way on the old abandoned road, which follows the modern road in general, but takes a more devious line through the landscape.

The uninhabited valley is called Glen More all the way, although you first follow the River Lussa upstream, then cross the watershed almost unawares on a peat bog and trace the River Colado downstream. On the left lies a tangled mass of mountains rising to 2,300ft (700m), interspersed

The ruined settlement at Gualachaolish broods over the narrows of Loch Spelve near the start of the Pilgrims' Way; beyond is the Firth of Lorn and the mainland

with lonely freshwater lochs and cold tarns that fill remote glacial holes in the rocks. These intransigent fists of granite are less visited than the set piece of Ben More and represent the remains of an ancient intrusion of volcanic magma up to the surface.

Visitors from England are at once struck by the peculiar rock formations on Mull, and if they are at all familiar with geology they will recognise an ancient volcanic landscape. Virtually the whole of Scotland, but especially the Highlands, has been subject to tremendous volcanic eruptions in the distant past. The western islands of Skye, Arran and Mull are all fascinating examples of extinct volcanoes and they have been intensively studied. In the case of Mull a huge central volcano flooded almost the whole island with Tertiary basalts – that

is, fine-grained basic lava with a dark grey colour. These flows extend across onto the mainland, forming the whole end of the Morvern peninsula. The volcano on Mull spewed and oozed its lavas from all kinds of side vents and a network of fissures around its base. Through some peculiarity deep in the earth's crust it also intruded two large bodies of acidic magma in the form of granite into the centre of the island. The larger one stretches from Salen to Glen More and forms the eastern part of the Ben More massif, which is neatly bordered on the south by an intrusion of gabbro, while the smaller and more contorted one forms the structures of Ben Buie and Creach Beinn south of Glen More. Only at the south-western tip did the older rocks survive this onslaught: the wonderful red granite forms a huge blob about 5 miles (8km) across on the end of the Ross of Mull. Across the Sound of Iona are the most stable structures in the area and some of the oldest rocks in the whole British Isles;

they are of pre-Cambrian age, over six hundred million years old. A final peculiarity is the lovely green-veined Iona marble which, along with other rocks metamorphosed by the intense heat of the volcano, is found in small quantities and is greatly prized by pilgrims to Iona.

Should the weather be favourable for climbing Ben More, the usual place to start from on this side is the bridge over the Allt Teanga Brideig (NM 564307). A footpath leads straight up to the summit ridge. From here onwards the Pilgrims' Way along the old road down the Ross of Mull is prominently marked by a series of five ancient standing stones, each one marked on the Ordnance Survey maps. No one knows how many stones there were originally, but the survivors have been systematically adapted to Christian use by the incision of a cross. Megaliths are found widely on Mull: the best example is the Lochbuie stone circle and outlying menhirs (NM 617251) that stand in a flat field, but are concealed from their surroundings by gorse, near Moy Castle. According to Professor Alexander Thom, the expert on megalithic astronomy, the circle was an important solar observatory.

On the shore just beyond Pennyghael (NM 507263) is a cairn about 87yd (80m) from the road. On top is a stone cross commemorating the Beaton family, the famous Ollamnh Muileach, or Mull doctors, whose great skill lay in the use of herbs. They came originally from Béthune in Burgundy and were physicians first to the lords of the isles and then to the Macleans of Duart.

The road crosses a landscape that was formed entirely by Tertiary basalt flows, where crags and odd steps often break through the turf and peat cover. Then between the hamlet of Bunessan and Ardfenaig is a zone of mica schist, another metamorphic rock, before the glorious red granite on the tip of Ross of Mull. Our route drops down finally into the ferry settlement of Fionnphort, a place of astonishing blandness that squats on the colourful and wild rocky shore.

The Adventurers' Path

Most visitors to Mull will be loath to confine themselves to a mere 670ft (205m) in such a spectacular landscape. From the summit of Ben More (3,170ft/ 966m), on a clear day you can see practically the whole of the Hebrides – at least fifty islands. The temptation to ignore history temporarily in favour of romance can be strong. So you will find on the map a suggested Adventurers' Path across Mull which takes in the two highest mountains and the best of the coastline.

In climbing terms Mull cannot compare with the Cuillins of Skye, but it does offer some extremely challenging and exhilarating walking. In particular it offers the only 'Munro' on an island, apart from those on Skye. Munros are those isolated Scottish peaks which rise to over 3,000ft (914m), and they are named after the Victorian climber Sir Hugh Munro. The definition of an isolated peak is difficult, but authorities generally give the accolade to a total of 279 mountains.

Following this Adventurers' Path will require settled weather both to enjoy the scenery and to avoid a nasty case of exposure. Complying with the conventional wisdom about the best time of year in the Highlands, the exploration for this chapter was scheduled for May. A glorious May it turned out to be, calm and warm with just the occasional cloud for scenic effect. In the remote sunny coves it was a moot point who was enjoying themselves more, the human explorers or the pink thrift flowering in the rocky crevices. They say that the later summer

Scarcely a path now leads to the remote ruined church at Killean above Rubha na Cille ('point of the burying ground'), once the subject of its own papal indulgences

was awful, so you have been warned! Atrocious weather in the Western Isles can put anyone in a bad mood, even the dedicated early Munro-bagger Dr John MacCulloch, who abominated Mull as 'a detestable island; trackless and repulsive, rude without beauty, stormy, rainy and dreary'.

The Adventurers' Path gives an even better feeling for the landscape of Mull than the lowland route of the pilgrims. It crosses the whole island from north to south and from east to west, with unforgettable views along all the arms of this spidery island. The climber Hamish Brown described Mull in the following way:

> The hills were hazy with the sweet reek of burning and when we passed the source of the scent, by Loch Scridain, it was replaced by the tang of the sea. There had been curlews and wheatears in the glen, here oystercatchers and redshank added their calls. It was full spring and suddenly this felt home – where sun and sea and mountains meet, westwards where all dreams lie.

The enduring memory of Mull is one of rugged and tawny brown mountains rising across the other side of a long sea loch. My favourite memory was not Ben More but a mountain called Bearraich: for three days I admired its splendid low profile ringed by cliffs of columnar basalt, but I never reached it.

The path begins at the ferry terminal in the picturesque harbour of Tobermory (Mary's Well), Mull's only village.

Nothing could be more picturesque than the situation of this little harbour, which is surrounded by the most dramatic islands and inlets imaginable. The brightly painted houses along the quayside have achieved widespread chocolate-box fame and are truly delightful. There are numerous places to stay, including a youth hostel; it is best to contact the information centre in Main Street. You should then look for the Tobermory Treasure: the story goes that a galleon of the Spanish Armada, laden with fabulous wealth to pay the troops, exploded mysteriously while anchored in the harbour.

The path follows the unfenced little road towards Dervaig through Forestry Commission plantations as far as the freshwater Loch Carnain

an Amais, where it climbs the ridge parallel to Loch Frisa over the summits of Speinne More (1,456ft/444m) and Speinne Beag (1,158ft/353m), descending through more conifers to the ruinous ancient chapel (Cill an Ailein) and rock (NM 545455) near Aros where Columba himself preached. From here the track swings down to the sea, where there is a fine well-drained spot for camping (NM 537413) with good views down the length of Loch na Keal. From here the path follows the south shore of the loch as far as Dhiseig farm (NM 496357), where an easy route up Ben More begins.

The little burn which waters the farm, Abhainn Dhiseig, takes you almost to the top, so it is impossible to get lost on the way up. Rough scree-covered slopes cover the whole top of Ben More. Without a good sense of balance these chutes of disintegrating Tertiary basalt can be tricky to descend. Scree-running is a lot of fun until you get to the bigger boulders at the bottom and find you cannot stop!

It will be best to have with you not just the large-scale map essential for tackling Ben More, but also one at a smaller scale. If the weather is clear the view extends at least 60 miles (96km) in all directions and it is likely to take a most enjoyable hour to sort out the fifty islands which are visible, and the jumbled confusion of Munros on the mainland.

You should be warned that several ridges radiate from the summit of Ben More and if it is misty you must pick the right one very carefully, for the top of the mountain is highly magnetic and can cause an error of 180° in a compass bearing. One popular way down is along the knife ridge eastwards to Ben More's subsidiary summit, A'Chioch. Where the path drops down into the glen leading north-east to Glen Ba, turn south-east to reach the path on the left bank of the Allt Teanga Brideig. This brings you to the narrow road along Glen More, the A849. It is also possible to take a short-cut off the summit, descending the corrie on the east side of Beinn nan Gobhar. Aim then for the prehistoric standing stone (NM 547300) which marks the old course of the Pilgrims' Way. From here the Adventurers' Path gets tamer but no less dramatic, detouring via another very rough path along a lonely and fantastic stretch of coastline. Continue first along the

Fionnphort road past another ancient standing stone (NM 544282) and the Kinloch Inn, turning left into Glen Leidle at Pennyghael. Eventually this twisting lane drops steeply down past Inniemore Lodge, a long-established summer school of painting, into Carsaig Bay.

If you are following this path in sections with a car, abandon the wheels here and follow the rough but level track westwards along the foreshore. The rock formations are really splendid: slippery slate beds which are covered at high tide, support soft sandstone overlain by irregular cliffs of columnar basalt nearly 656ft (200m) thick. The footpath has all but disappeared by the time you reach the Nuns' Cave (NM 523204), a deep triangular cave in the sandstone cliffs that was used centuries ago by the Iona monks as a workshop for carving the grey slaty slabs from the foreshore outside. On the left wall three or four of their crosses can be seen, inscribed on the wall in idle moments by the monks.

On the Ross of Mull near Bunessan we see Tertiary basalt flows from Mull's great volcano, while across Loch Scridain lies Bearraich, ringed by columnar basalt cliffs

This was a famous school of carving, both for the ornamental stonework of the abbey and its burial ground, as well as further afield. The cave's name stems from a brief episode: when the nuns were expelled from Iona during the Reformation they found shelter here for a while.

From the Nuns' Cave the going becomes even rougher: you can continue for about 2 miles (3km) along the foot of the cliffs to the spectacular Carsaig Arches. Here the columnar basalts descend to the sea and are worn into arches, caves and other weird shapes.

There is no way through Carsaig Arches, but the recommended way out ascends the cliff diagonally to the left of the Nuns' Cave. So easy is this straight grassy path up a natural cleft that it is known as the

Nuns' Pass. It no longer connects with a proper track, but our path continues along Gleann Alasgaig and Gleann Airigh na Searsain, to connect with the Pilgrims' Way on the shores of Loch Scridain for the final stretch to Iona.

We have now met Mull's columnar basalts, at Bearraich from a distance and at Carsaig at first hand, so this is a good place to remind you that you are within striking distance of the most famous specimen in the British Isles: Staffa of Fingal's Cave and Mendelssohn fame. A lovely wooden fishing boat leaves every day, weather permitting, from the quays on both sides of the Sound of Iona. In calm weather and at high tide the tight-lipped Mr Kirkpatrick shoots right into the cave on a wave to land his human cargo among the magnificent dark grey columns. The huge hexagonal crystals of basalt lava were formed when the lava cooled ex-

The wild walk along Mull's south coast is rewarded by finding the deep Nun's Cave above the foreshore: until the Reformation it formed the principle workshop used by the monks of Iona Abbey for carving stone memorials

tremely slowly in extensive thick sheets. People also go to Staffa to see the puffins: you can crawl within a few feet of them on the cliff-tops at the other end of the island.

· THE SACRED ISLAND OF IONA ·

The Earliest Monastery

During the Bronze Age Iona was a minor centre of an ancient religion – nearby at Lochbuie on Mull lies one of the major astronomically aligned stone circles of prehistoric Scotland. But when the first monks came here in 563 it appears that Iona was uninhabited and Dun Bhuirg, a small hillfort on the west coast, was long abandoned.

The monks first marked off an area of church land – part of this rectangular boundary ditch (about 1,100 × 500ft (335 × 152m) can still be seen turning a corner north-west of the present abbey. Then they constructed a set of temporary buildings from timber, wattle and daub: a church, cells for the individual brethren, and perhaps communal structures like workshops, an infirmary, a refectory, a

dormitory for novices and a guest-house. Farm buildings would have been outside the boundary ditch. The island affords a good supply of hard volcanic building stone, including the red granite which was carried across by glaciers from the Ross of Mull. So it is likely that within Columba's lifetime, or after one of the Viking raids, the monks gave their buildings a more permanent form, even if their architecture seems very crude by later medieval standards.

We can still get an idea of what the early monastery on Iona might have looked like, at Skellig Michael, a wild and wonderful rock screaming with thousands of seabirds in the open Atlantic swell 15 miles (24km) off the coast of County Kerry, Ireland. Here another group of Celtic monks came to live in the sixth century, ever anxious to find a yet harsher place for their meditation. Cut off from the rest of mankind for weeks at a time by Atlantic storms and presumably existing on little besides prayer and puffins' eggs, these ascetic hermits built on their astonishing eyrie a set of drystone 'beehive' cells with simple corbelled roofs called *clochans,* which the wind and rain have still not destroyed.

The Viking Intervention

The golden age of the Celts was not to last, for in 790 the Vikings first sacked Lindisfarne. The undefended monasteries along the coasts were easy targets, with their collections of church plate and other wealth. Soon Norsemen in their longships invaded the Western Isles, attacking Iona in 795 and destroying the monastery, then repeating this raid in 802, 806 and 825. Although the local community recovered partially from each of these blows, many of the monks withdrew to the Columban monastery at Kells in County Meath, taking some of their treasures with them. This is how the famous Columban illuminated manuscript, the *Book of Kells,* came to Ireland. Iona's greatest devastation came in 986 when the raiders found the shrine of St Columba and his bones, but not the treasure they wanted. According to tradition the Norsemen threw the shrine and its relics into the sea and it came ashore in Ireland at Downpatrick, where the abbot recognised it by

St Columba's Abbey on Iona in about 1500. The island of Mull lies across the sound

divine intervention – and so Columba is now said to rest there alongside St Patrick himself. The relics may thus have survived the destruction of the Celtic monastery.

Reconstruction

An English writer tells us that in the eleventh century, Queen Margaret, wife of Malcolm Canmore, rebuilt the monastery and gave the monks royal support; the simple St Oran's Chapel in the burial ground dates from this time. Another century passed before the next phase: Reginald, famous laird of the Clan Donald, built the splendid Benedictine abbey some time between 1164 and 1203, and the nearby Augustinian nunnery was constructed soon after. The abbey enjoyed several partial rebuildings, principally around 1450, but the style remained that of 1200. After the dis-

solution of the monasteries, all these conventual buildings fell into disrepair.

Today the nunnery remains in a picturesque state of decay, while the abbey has been beautifully restored during the first seventy years of the twentieth century by the Iona Community. Each part of the monastery has been carefully rebuilt using the same stone and the same style as the masons used in the Middle Ages. The hard and newly cut stone still looks so fresh and sharp that at quiet times of the day, the last five centuries seem not to have passed at all.

Where was Columba's Shrine?

Where exactly did St Columba's relics lie during their two and a half centuries on his island? They were probably not in the reconstructed chapel just outside the west door of the present Benedictine church. This oratory's modern name – St Columba's Shrine – is an evident misnomer, for the eighth-century shrine containing his remains almost certainly stood in the principal church of the monastery. It is very unusual for an important shrine to be anywhere but at the eastern end of a major church, let alone actually outside it.

Route 4

THE ROAD TO THE ISLE: THE MAINLAND TO IONA

ROUTE LENGTH: 35½/41 miles (57/66km) · MAPS: OS 1:50,000 Nos 47, 48, 49

ACCOMMODATION

Hotel and bed and breakfast accommodation are available in Tobermory and at settlements all over the island of Mull – contact the Information Office to arrange bookings: tel: (0631) 3122/3551. There are youth hostels at Oban and Tobermory. The Iona Community welcomes Christians of all denominations and now has extensive accommodation: tel: 06817 404. If they are full they can recommend bed and breakfast accommodation on Iona.

BANKING FACILITIES

Only at Tobermory with the exception of a mobile bank.

ISOLATED PUBLIC TELEPHONES

Map ref	Location of Telephone	Map ref	Location of Telephone
NM 557447	Aros	NM 517264	Pennyghael
NM 546407	Gruline, junction of B8073/B8035	NM 540220	Carsaig
NM 728333	Head of Loch Don	NM 404230	Knockan

VILLAGES OR HAMLETS WITH GENERAL STORES

Tobermory, Dervaig, Salen, Craignure, Pennyghael, Bunessan, Fionnphort, Iona.

TOURIST INFORMATION OFFICES

Oban, Tobermory.

5

THE WELSH WAY
through Pembrokeshire

ost of Pembrokeshire is rolling country-side, which is both pleasant and productive. Central to its development in Christian times was the settlement by Normans, Flemings and the English. This occurred mostly in the south of the county, giving rise to the name Anglia Transwalliana (England beyond Wales): if you study the OS map for a moment you will find that you can draw a fairly sharp east-west boundary with Welsh place-names to the north and English to the south.

The Normans installed their bishop, Bernard, a clerk from the court, so as to obliterate the independent cells of the Celtic Church with a proper ecclesiastical chain of command. A series of Norman strongholds soon followed, and Henry I deliberately introduced a sizable colony of Flemings as the final stage in subjugating the Welsh.

The south of Pembrokeshire is often called Little England and its most characteristic building is the typical church tower, usually with a pronounced batter to the walls and always crowned with a corbelled-out parapet. Not surprisingly, the settlers built them as refuges, look-outs and beacons rolled into one. In many cases they are all that survives from before the frequent nineteenth-century rebuilding of the rest of the church, their drab grey surfaces often mottled with white and yellow lichen, mosses and ferns. Under the settlers the woollen industry prospered; but the Welsh 'voted with their feet' by leaving for the north of the county.

However, once in the western peninsula called Dewisland (David's Land) – and the boundary is usually taken as the line from Fishguard to Treffgarne – the landscape undergoes a remarkable change, which may seem like a step back in time. Gerald of Wales, a great traveller and chronicler in the twelfth century and a local man, wrote of it: 'Menevia [St David's] . . . the soil stony and barren, neither clothed with woods, distinguished by rivers, nor adorned by meadows, ever exposed to the winds and the tempests'. Few places on the British mainland have preserved an appearance and atmosphere so substantially unchanged since medieval times. Visitors who have been to the remote Gaeltacht of County Kerry in south-west Ireland may recognise the spirit of that ancient landscape in the turf-clad stone walls here. A Victorian traveller called E. A. Kilner understood Dewisland; writing in 1891 he said of it:

There were few alien settlers, and to this day it is a district purely Celtic, contrasting markedly with the people of the south of Pembrokeshire. They speak the old language – a service in Welsh in the cathedral is unique and striking – and they preserve the type of character, manners, and appearance of their ancestors. Prosperous farmsteads dot the undulating and almost treeless country . . . Breaking the monotony of outline are curious bosses of trap rock, which, like silent giants, frown over the fields.

Historically Dewisland is the oldest lordship in Wales, descending for centuries in unbroken possession of the original heirs. This succession supposedly goes back to pre-Norman times, although only post-Conquest records remain. Whatever its history, for us it has a wild and spiritual beauty that is found nowhere else in Wales.

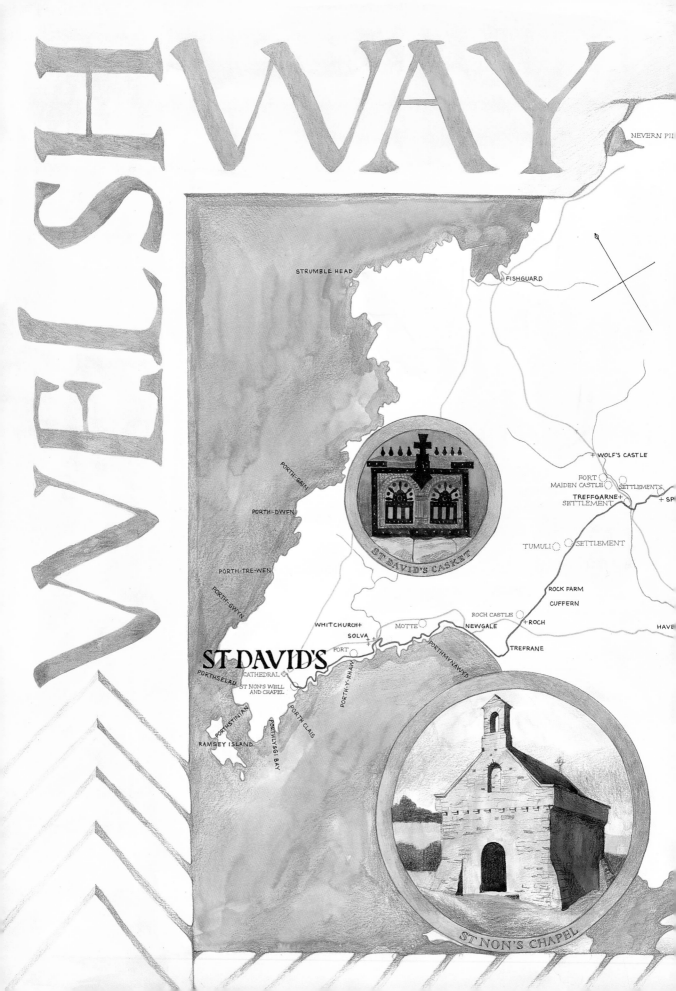

WELSH

FISH WAY

NEVERN PI

STRUMBLE HEAD

+ FISHGUARD

WOLF'S CASTLE

FORT
MAIDEN CASTLE

SETTLEMENTS

TREFFGARNE +
SETTLEMENT

+ SP

PORTH-GAIN

TUMULI

SETTLEMENT

PORTH-DWEN

ST DAVID'S CASKET

ROCK FARM

CUFFERN

PORTH-TRE-WEN

ROCH CASTLE

PORTH-SWIN

WHITCHURCH +

MOTTE

NEWGALE

+ ROCH

HAVE

SOLVA

PORTH-Y-RHAW

PORTHMYNAWYD

TREFRANE

ST DAVID'S

CATHEDRAL +

FORT

PORTHSELAU

ST NON'S WELL
AND CHAPEL

PORTHSTINIAN

PORTH CLAIS

PORTHLYSGI BAY

RAMSEY ISLAND

ST NON'S CHAPEL

LLANFIHANGEL TO ST DAVID'S

KILOMETRES
MILES

New Town
St Clears
Old Town
REMAINS OF CHURCH
REMAINS OF CHURCH

AFON COWIN

WHITLAND ABBEY
INSCRIBED STONE
PILGRIM STONES
LLANFIHANGEL

LLANFALLTEG
RHYDYWRACH
LLANDDOWROR

CASTLE
LAUGHARNE

AFON TAF

WHITLAND

TUMULUS

LAMPETER VALE

MESTEAD
CLARBESTON
BETHESDA

KNOCK FARM

CASTLE
LLAWHADEN

NARBERTH
CASTLE

RUINS OF
PILGRIM HOSPICE

HOLYWELL
SENTENCE CASTLE

SLEBECH
COMMANDERY OF KNIGHTS HOSPITALLER

NEYLAND

CASTLE
PEMBROKE

PILGRIM'S GRAVESTONES, LLANFIHANGEL

THE WELSH WAY
Llanfihangel Abercowin to St David's Cathedral

The Roads to St David's

As many as half of the pilgrims who travelled to St David's shrine came by sea, from north Wales, Ireland, Cornwall and Brittany, passing the dangerous rocks in large coracles. Working in with the tide they would hope to land at the harbour of Porthclais, where the monks built a breakwater. Pilgrims would then pass St Non's Well and Chapel and Whitewell Chapel on their short journey into the city. But should they misjudge the landing, or the tide prove difficult, there were plenty of alternative landing places for a light boat, even on such a rocky Atlantic coastline as this. All around the peninsula the bays each have their pilgrim chapel to welcome the seafarers: Porthlysgi: Capel y Pistyll; Porthstinian: St Justinian's Chapel; Porthselau: Capel Cwmwdig, and Porthmawr: St Patrick's Chapel.

Travellers on foot came from two main directions. Pilgrims doing the grand tour of Welsh shrines and holy wells might come from St Winefrede's Well in Flintshire, north Wales (see Chapter 9), via Strata Florida Abbey in Cardiganshire, before merging with the palmers from the English Midlands. Once in Pembrokeshire they would reach the important resting place of Nevern where a fine pilgrim cross and numerous ancient funerary crosses are still to be seen. On their last day these pilgrims would follow the north coast into Dewisland, a distance from Nevern of some 22 miles (35km).

However, the route chosen to reach St David's shrine is the southerly road from a now obscure parish called Llanfihangel Abercowin, some 44 miles (71km), or two days' walking, from his city. One reason for this choice will become apparent when you read the unique legend about Llanfihangel Abercowin (see p81). Another reason is that the path links up more historic sites and monuments than the northerly route, including the rare ruins of a pilgrims' hospice and the bishop of St David's castle. Thirdly, we can walk the final stretch along one of the finest lengths of the

The Cambrian rocks on this headland called Dinas Fach are some of the oldest on the British mainland; they overlook the wide St Bride's Bay on the Pembrokeshire coast path

Pembrokeshire coastline, from Newgale Sands to St Non's Well.

In actual fact, the choice is not as simple, because the distribution of old hospice sites, including one belonging to the Knights Hospitaller (at Slebech) and one to the Knights Templar (Sentence Castle at Templeton) and a third one at Tavernspite (ie spittal, that is, hospital), indicates that some travellers took a more southerly route still. These pilgrims would have passed through Haverfordwest itself, centre of English power in the county, and rejoined our stream at Roch Castle. But today's pilgrim would find this route, which often follows the modern A40 trunk road carrying the heavy traffic to Haverfordwest, Milford Haven and Fishguard, an unpleasant walk.

The Life and Cult of St David

David, or Dewi Sant in Welsh, is the patron saint of Wales who gave his name to the peninsula, Dewisland, where his shrine, cathedral and city may be found. It is difficult to ascertain the truth about the historical David, however, because we cannot be certain whether the information written about his life by later chroniclers, such as Rhygyfarch of Llanbadarn Fawr in the eleventh century, is distortion or sheer invention passed down from father to son. As with the life of St Patrick, there is an almost complete lack of contemporary witness.

We know for certain that David was a native Welshman who lived in the sixth century, and that he was a great missionary and founder of monasteries in his country. He is said to have come from a princely line. His father was Sant, son of Ceredig, founder of the kingdom of Cardigan (Ceredigion). According to Rhygyfarch's *Life of St David*, his mother was St Non, a nun at Ty Gwyn near Whitesand Bay, Dyfed, who was seduced by Prince Sant and then spent the rest of her life in prayer and self-mortification. However, it is possible that she became a nun in widowhood after David's birth, which, according to tradition, took place at St Non's Well (on our route). Non retired to Brittany and died there, where her fine tomb survives at Dirinion.

Miracles surround the stories of David's life: Rhygyfarch even supposes that an oracle foretold

Celtic hermit's cell such as St David would have known, based on surviving examples on Skellig Michael, a remote rock in the open Atlantic off the coast of County Kerry

his birth by thirty years to Prince Sant. At his baptism a fountain of the purest water burst forth spontaneously for the rite (this is now St Non's Well), while a blind monk who was holding the infant miraculously received his sight. David was brought up at Hen Fynyw, probably in Cardiganshire. After founding monasteries all over the land, he chose Vallis Rosina for his main community, which grew into the influential monastery and diocese of St David's. The smoke from the saint's first fire at Vallis Rosina is supposed to have so angered the powerful local Druid and chieftain Boia, that a miracle was required to prevent the murder of David and his acolytes.

He is buried in his own monastery of St David's, and, remarkably, his medieval shrine still survives on the north side of the presbytery. During the Reformation an ancient oak and iron reliquary containing his bones was hidden in a niche behind the cathedral's high altar and was only rediscovered during Victorian restoration work. On each St David's Day (1 March) the cathedral chapter decorates the niche and its casket with daffodils in honour of its founder.

Nothing is known of the early buildings erected by David and his followers: probably they resembled the earliest wattle and daub monasteries at Iona and Lindisfarne. We know that the first church burnt down in 645 and that the Danes sacked the buildings in 1078, killing Bishop Abraham.

Early manuscripts make clear that by the tenth century David was already regarded as the patron saint and standard bearer of the Welsh. When the first Norman bishop, Bernard, totally reorganised the community he had to apply for approval by the Pope, Callixtus II. This he secured in a document of 1123, confirming his privileges as bishop of the church of St Andrew and St David – for David this was an instrument tantamount to the modern process of canonisation. The document also confirmed the great spiritual importance that had already been achieved by St David's shrine, by granting that two pilgrimages to St David's were considered equal to one pilgrimage to Rome, or in Latin, *Roma semel quantum, Dat bic Menevia tantum.*

Even before St David's had been granted spiritual recognition by Rome, it had received its first visit from an English king: in 1081 William the Conqueror came, nominally in the spirit of pilgrimage, but actually on a military reconnaissance to investigate the possibility of launching an invasion of Ireland from Dewisland. Then Henry II visited the cathedral in 1171, on his return from his bloody campaign in Ireland and only a few months after the tragic murder of Thomas Becket. Other royal visits followed in due course: Edward I, the king who finally subdued Wales, and Queen Eleanor, Edward III and Queen Philippa, and possibly also King John. Henry's royal gifts and those of the rising tide of pilgrims at this time brought immense wealth to the cathedral, so that an ambitious rebuilding programme began in 1178 and continued unabated for three centuries, leaving us the cathedral, its precinct and fine gatehouse, and the splendid Bishop's Palace across the little River Alun – a magnificent ensemble which is unrivalled in Britain.

During Victorian times when the architect George Gilbert Scott saved the tower from collapse in a fifteen-year programme of sensitive restoration, St David's and its cathedral were remote. Even God's Wonderful Railway, as the GWR was known, never approached closer than a dozen miles to the isolated town, as its interests lay in the docks at Fishguard and Milford Haven; neither has the motor car had much effect on the ancient splendour of the cathedral precinct. Where most British cathedrals suffer from swirling smelly traffic, St David's has preserved almost alone a welcome sense of peace.

The Start at Llanfihangel Abercowin

The old church stands where the waters of the Afon Taf and the Afon Cowin meet. The dedication to the Archangel Michael is often found in areas that were important for pagan worship (see Chapter 3), and it may be significant that at least four prehistoric stones stand nearby on the banks of the Cowin. The place-name is highly descriptive, for Llanfihangel Abercowin is simply Welsh for 'the holy place of St Michael by the mouth of the River Cowin'. Confusion can arise because in 1848 the parish church was moved 2½ miles (4km) northwards to a new site on the present main road to Haverfordwest which was easier for people to reach. The old church (SN 303134) is five minutes' walk south-east from the farm Trefenty, close to the remains of a motte and bailey castle, a pilgrims' lodge and a once-important crossing point of the Afon Cowin. On the other side of the little river there is evidence that this road was used by pilgrims, in the form of the place-name Pilgrims' Rest. Now there is just an isolated farm on the site of this supposed hospice, but in an adjacent field may be found the ruins of Llandilo-abercowin, or 'the church of St Teilo by the mouth of the River Cowin'. St Teilo was a companion of St David, later Bishop of Llandaff, a very popular Welsh saint.

The most romantic evidence for this pilgrimage route is the remarkable and pathetic story attached to the old church at Llanfihangel Abercowin, a story so peculiar that we start our pilgrimage here rather that at another monument further on. The legend has gathered around what are known as the five Pilgrim Stones in the churchyard. A band of destitute pilgrims are said to have arrived here in the last stages of exhaustion. Driven to desperation they resolved on a suicide pact to avoid perishing from hunger. The three graves which they dug for themselves under the ancient yew tree are supposed to belong to a mason, a glazier and a ropemaker, while the remaining pair lie close at hand, but now rather overgrown, by the churchyard wall. Popular tradition asserts that it is only necessary to keep these tombstones clear of weeds for the peninsula to be free of reptiles – furthermore, if this duty is neglected the surrounding landowners will lose their property.

When opened, the middle grave of the three was found to contain several shells, possibly indicating that the corpse did in fact belong to a pilgrim. What kernel of truth, though, gave rise to the bizarre legend of the five pilgrims it is now impossible to tell. Such tales invite incredulity: readers might like to consider why pilgrims with strength enough to dig their own graves did not beg for alms along the road. The shapes of the gravestones, the figure sculpture and the design of the ornament point to a date around 1200 – that is, around the time of the foundation of the church, where similar tool-marks made by axes occur on the chancel arch. The sculpture on two of the graves shows knightly attributes and at least two of the figures are female. In 1912 the inspector of the Royal Commission on Historical Monuments visited the graves and made the following conclusion: 'It is fairly manifest that the gravestones are memorials to persons who were connected with, and probably lived at, the mound and bailey castle a few hundred yards away.' We shall never know whether this conclusion is correct, but the romantic legend remains unique.

The church moved to a new site and within a few generations the old church had become roofless and decayed. Now, although the nave walls still stand to nearly full height and the tower retains most of three storeys, ivy overruns the structure and farm stock wanders into the church and the graveyard.

The Route to St David's

From the ruined church at Llanfihangel Abercowin follow the footpath north-west past Trefenty farm (the name means the House of Fenty) into the old town of St Clears. An important Cluniac priory once stood on the site and its church is now used by the parish. The church has a wonderful Norman chancel arch with three orders of carving. The house was governed directly from Cluny and served by foreign monks, which led Henry V to suppress it as an 'alien priory' during the Hundred Years' War. The Normans fortified the town: a large motte still looms above High Street.

Crossing the Afon Taf by the bridge at the bottom of High Street, a lane leads to Llanddowror (the name means Church of St Towror). Two

'Pilgrim Stones' stand upright in a field on the west side of the churchyard. It is common in Wales to find curious and ancient stones near or built into churches – there are the remains of a Bronze Age stone circle next to St Non's Chapel at the end of this route.

A track leads through the woods up the right bank of the river and after 2 miles (3km) crosses by a little bridge (SN 237161) near Dolerwydd. After passing on a lane under the railway before Pont-y-Fenni the route briefly joins the main A40 before following a footpath north between the two Regwm farmhouses and then west.

Whitland Abbey is a famous historical site also known as Alba Domus. Here Hywel Dda (Howel the Good) summoned a company of clerics and laymen to declare and confirm provisions of Welsh customary law in the tenth century. The few fragments of the Cistercian abbey found among the orchards indicate a rebuilding phase in about 1200. The foundations have not been excavated. The unpretentious Victorian country house now bearing the name Whitland Abbey doubtless incorporates much of the medieval stonework.

Next to the abbey a ford and footbridge cross the little stream and a very stony track leads away to Cwmfelin Boeth. Then a delightful series of lanes leads westwards through the quiet farmland, past the tiny settlements of Rhydywrach, Llanfallteg and Bethesda as far as the Eastern Cleddau.

Llawhaden church lies at the foot of the hill in a secluded position by the river. The exceptionally beautiful building has a steeply pitched roof and a strongly fortified tower. Llawhaden Castle protected the surrounding rich estates which belonged to the bishops of St David's. In about 1300 Bishop Martin lavished enormous expenditure on transforming the old castle into a luxurious fortified palace. Here the wealthy prelates entertained their important guests in style. Among the impressive walls and towers you can find the quarters of the permanent garrison – a rare survival in any castle. The bishops also maintained palaces at Lamphey near Pembroke and at St David's itself; both of them are worth visiting.

The ruins of the medieval pilgrim hospice stand in a field on the south-west side of Llawhaden

Llawhaden Castle was long a possession of the bishops of St David's: this massive gateway dates from 1300 when Bishop Martin converted the castle to a luxurious palace

village. Although the rubble walls are much battered, the corbelled stone roof of the hall remains, romantically covered with grass and ivy. According to a charter in the British Library, the energetic builder Bishop Beck founded the hospital in 1287. Just one custodian, known as a prior, looked after the guests.

Very quiet walled lanes lead across the railway to Clarbeston: the Victorian rebuilding of the ancient church in its raised graveyard has preserved the typical Pembrokeshire tower, which tapers upwards to a projecting embattled parapet. Then a purposeful lane heads for Spittal. The name indicates that a hospital once stood here to shelter the pilgrims. Again the founder was Bishop Beck; much of it was pulled down in about 1870 to build a farmhouse and today nothing of the hospital remains. The grey slate church, restored in 1861 and 1898, stands in an ancient graveyard; inside is a scalloped Norman font and a hagioscope (an internal window to view the altar) on either side of the chancel. Near here, in 1572, was found a

monastic treasure trove of gold and silver in a black 'crockle', which was duly reported by John Wogan, the High Sheriff of Pembrokeshire, to Lord Burghley.

The Western Cleddau is where we cross the border and enter Dewisland. The whole plateau has a spiritual feel to it, one that is both ascetic as well as exciting. Perhaps that is why no king ever fortified it.

Treffgarne church was rebuilt on old foundations in 1850-75. Its position is peculiar in that it stands exactly where the lane from the west makes its first sharp turn for 5½ miles (9km). From Treffgarne we now follow this very pretty old lane, in parts just a bridleway; it is always bounded by ancient stone walls and keeps to the same line across the Dewisland plateau.

Roch Castle, a thirteenth-century peel tower, is

dramatically sited above the plateau on a crag of volcanic rock – which also bursts inconveniently through into the lower storey. Despite this the interior now provides a comfortable Edwardian country residence. In medieval times the pilgrims on the more southerly road through Haverfordwest would join our route here.

Follow the lane down past Trefrane onto Newgale Sands. From here we join the Pembrokeshire Coast Path. This is a wild and dramatic section which enjoys fine views, comparable in this book only with the walk along the north coast of Cornwall. From Newgale the walker must tackle some steep ups and downs along the well-marked and well-trodden path to Solva, a pretty haven for pleasure boats which has pubs, shops and a café. From Solva to the popular beach in Caerfai Bay the

Following this old road westwards to Roch Castle, our pilgrims would here meet others from Haverfordwest

path is comparatively overgrown and sometimes eroded, which could prove tricky in bad weather. After the beach the path improves, but the coastline becomes even wilder, with bold patches of yellow gorse, and daffodils flowering in time for St David's Day in sheltered spots. Ramsey Island dominates the view out to sea and is now an important bird sanctuary.

During the Middle Ages, pilgrims would have travelled on a road slightly inland, and detours will bring you to the sites they passed. Whitchurch once had a pilgrim hospice, but today is a hamlet with a slate-built church, now grotesquely stripped and whitewashed inside. In front of the churchyard gate is the stump of a cross called Maen Dewi (St David's Stone). Llandruidion is a farming hamlet where there was once another pilgrim hospice.

In St Non's Bay we reach an old landing place of the pilgrims at a place almost as holy as the cathedral. Here is the ruined St Non's Chapel, traditionally the site of St David's birth, and still showing work from as early as the seventh century, in particular a crudely carved Latin ring cross in the south-west corner. When the time came for the baby David to be christened, a spring suddenly and miraculously gushed forth so the ceremony could take place; this is now the Holy Well of St Non, in a much-hallowed deep slate niche near the chapel, with stone benches around it for visitors. The large house on the headland is now a retreat run by the Passionist Fathers. In the garden is an interesting chapel. Although built as recently as 1934, it is carefully modelled on the medieval chapels which formerly stood by the little havens all around St David's Head, and it actually incorporates stones gathered from ruined cottages which had in turn been made from stones robbed from Whitewell Priory.

At the holy Whitewell was a pilgrims' hospice (SM 751249) on the way from St Non's Bay into the little city. Bishop Beck, who held the see from 1280 to 1293, founded the 'hospitium'. The well supplied the Deanery with water. An entry in the diary of the Rev Francis Kilvert dated October 1871 reads: 'And so we came to the end of the world where the patron saint of Wales sleeps by the Western sea'.

The Shrine at the World's End

Pilgrims arriving on the Llawhaden road would reach the little city, which has always been unwalled, and might well have wondered where the cathedral was situated; for the city – which is no more than a village – is on the Dewisland plateau, while the cathedral is hidden, at the bottom of the Alun glen. Pilgrims would enter the cathedral precincts by the Tower Gate, and see the view that is shown in the watercolour on p86. No one has described the spirit of this remote place better than Jan Morris, in her book *The Matter of Wales:*

> It is the fourth holy building to stand upon the site . . . and has fine things to show the sightseer: a gorgeous roof of Irish oak, monumental pillars, quaintly carved misericords, memorials to long-dead bishops, bequests of forgotten grandees. Visitors sensitive to numen, though, will hardly notice these things, for the most compelling element of the building is something much more ethereal, a tremulous combination of light, hush and muted colour. The light is the sea-light that

St Non's Chapel, near an old landing place for sea-born pilgrims, gives a good idea of the probable appearance of the medieval pilgrim chapels around St David's

> comes through the windows, pale, watery and unclear; the colour is a purplish, drifting kind of colour, almost tangible, emanating perhaps from the stone of the walls; and the hush is the unmistakable pause of holiness.

Whether visitors are Welsh patriots or not, they should try to attend a service in the Welsh language in the cathedral. Such is the spirituality of the building and its setting that it matters not a whit that the lilting words are incomprehensible.

The remains of St David's shrine still exist, spared destruction during the Reformation. The shrine takes the form of a triple-arched stone screen built in 1275 to fill the gap between two Norman pillars on the north side of the presbytery. Originally it had a painted wooden canopy and panels showing St David, St Patrick and St Denis. The movable casket containing David's relics

The shrine at the world's end: St David's Cathedral and the Bishop's Palace in about 1340

rested on a shelf, but when strife threatened, an old order specified that it should be taken to safety one day's journey from the city. The Gothic niches under the shelf probably held other relics, while pilgrims would place their offerings in the holes on the rear of the shrine.

Only at Gloucester, Westminster, St Albans and Hereford do such complete remains survive from the numerous medieval shrines that once existed. The shrines at Gloucester and Westminster were those of Edward II and Henry VII, and as royal personages were spared by Henry VIII's commissioners. The shrine at St Albans was smashed, but the pieces survived and have been reassembled. Hereford's shrine of St Thomas de Cantelupe was spared by some unknown chance.

It is believed that St David's relics still exist in an ancient oak and iron casket which is now displayed in a stone niche behind the high altar – the very place where the clergy hid them in the sixteenth century. A beautiful wrought-iron screen thwarts latter-day relic stealers. If you want to see this shrine resplendent with daffodils you must visit the cathedral on St David's Day (1 March).

Route 5

THE WELSH WAY: LLANFIHANGEL ABERCOWIN TO ST DAVID'S CATHEDRAL

ROUTE LENGTH: 46 miles (74km) · MAPS: OS 1:50,000 Nos 157, 158, 159

PUBLIC HOUSES

Map ref	Name of Pub	Location
SN 277163	Black Lion**#	St Clears, near start of path
SN 110145	Angel**	High Street, Narberth, 2½ miles (4km) S of path
SM 957266	Wolfe's Castle***#	Wolfe, on A40, 1¼ miles (2km) N of Treffgarne
SM 848221	Duke of Edinburgh**#	Newgale
SM 805242	Ship**	Solva, on Pembrokeshire coastal path
SM 805242	Harbour House**	Solva, on Pembrokeshire coastal path
SM 750248	St Non's Hotel**#	St David's, on road from St Non's Well
SR 965946	St Govans**#	Bosherton, on detour to St Govan's Chapel

Key: *** Highly recommended by the *Good Pub Guide*   * Recommended
** Recommended by the *Good Pub Guide*   #Accommodation

VILLAGES OR HAMLETS WITH GENERAL STORES

St Clears, Llanddowror, Whitland, Narberth, Llawhaden, Clarbeston Road, Spittal, Treffgarne, Roch, Solva, St David's.

TOURIST INFORMATION OFFICES

Carmarthen, Whitland, St David's, Haverfordwest, Pembroke, Fishguard.

6

THE PATH TO HOLY ISLAND

L indisfarne, or Holy Island as it came to be called, lies off the coast of Northumberland. About a mile of tidal flats separate it from the mainland and the sea floods across twice a day, or in the words of an anonymous poet:

> For with the flow and ebb, its style
> Varies from continent to isle;
> Dry shod, o'er sands, twice every day,
> The pilgrims to the shrine find way;
> Twice every day the waves efface
> Of staves and sandelled feet the trace.

Clearly pilgrims could approach Lindisfarne from any landward direction, or indeed, from the sea if their helmsman knew the treacherous tides. In choosing a historically viable route which will be both attractive and interesting to travellers today, we must bear in mind the early development of the monastery, the settlement pattern in medieval Northumbria and the road system which existed.

In AD410 the Emperor Honorius renounced the Roman claim to control Britain in an edict advising the existing authorities to take steps for their own preservation. There is some evidence from coins minted after this event that Roman life continued at the town of Corstopitum, on the north bank of the Tyne between Hexham and Corbridge. It would be natural for native and Romanised Britons to withdraw into such towns for safety as the Anglian raiders from modern Denmark saw their chance and began to form permanent settlements.

In the North, as in much of Saxon England, a typical pattern developed, with the new settlers founding their villages near, but not directly on, the existing Roman roads, as a way of concealing their position from potential enemies. Neither the Angles nor the Saxons built any new strategic roads, so travellers in the early Middle Ages used the well-made and dense Roman network.

In this part of Northumbria there were two main Roman roads, both of which were probably built by Britain's governor, Agricola, during the first attempt to conquer Scotland in about AD80, or some forty years before the construction of Hadrian's Wall. Dere Street (occasionally called Watling Street) ran north from the legionary fortress and city at York (Eboracum) through Corbridge (Corstopitum) and then north-west into Scotland. Stanegate ran west from Corstopitum to the army base at Carlisle (Luguvalium).

There was also a third road from Corstopitum, a minor route later known as the Devil's Causeway, which branched off to the north-east immediately after Dere Street passed through Hadrian's Wall by the Port Gate. This road may date from AD139, when the new emperor Antoninus Pius ordered the reoccupation of Scotland. The road passed the small Roman fort at Hartburn, a larger fort at Learchild (probably Alauna) that guarded the crossing of the River Aln, then Breamish fort above the hamlet of Powburn, and ended at the small fort of Springhill at the mouth of the River Tweed opposite Berwick. The road takes an easy line east of the main hills, reaching a maximum height of only 820ft (250m) on Longframlington Common.

The medieval pilgrims' way to Lindisfarne therefore followed the route along the ironically named Devil's Causeway, which was in use for centuries before the building of the Great North Road further east. Much of the charm of this route lies in the fact that long stretches have been abandoned for so long. Do not be deceived by the continuous line that is so clearly marked by the

Lindisfarne seen across the saltflats at low tide from the nature reserve at Fenwick. The birds are oystercatchers

Ordnance Survey. In many places you have to look hard to see traces of the agger, or bank, which is typically 40ft (12m) wide and flanked by broad ditches now only about 1ft (0.3m) deep, while sometimes it has been completely ploughed out and nothing can be seen from the ground. The neglect of this former highway has now reached the stage that, along its 42 miles (68km) from Hadrian's Wall to our turn-off for Lindisfarne, only 12 miles (19km) are a public right of way.

It is not my purpose to encourage readers to trespass on private property or to damage crops. Indeed, the last traveller to follow the whole line of the Devil's Causeway may have been Mr H. MacLauchlan who prepared a report on it in 1864 for the Duke of Northumberland under the title *A Survey of the Eastern Branch of Watling Street*. So the route shown on the map is one for walkers using rights of way, keeping always close to the Roman road if not actually following it, and linking all the points of medieval and religious interest along the way. During the Middle Ages, pilgrims would also have left the Roman road to stay at inns, hospices or priories, and to visit shrines along the way.

One of the most striking features of this beautiful and lonely landscape is the severe depopulation which has occurred since the Middle Ages. Large fields of ridge and furrow can be seen almost everywhere and show where crops once grew, although often the nearest modern settlement is miles away. Neither will you have to look far to see traces of the deserted villages: Bywell, Bolam and Edlingham are three examples. Rural Northumberland now has just three market towns and perhaps five proper villages, where once there were scores. Other habitation consists of scattered hamlets, farmhouses and cottages. Without doubt, this is the largest tract of deeply quiet countryside in England.

PATH

TO HOLY ISLAN

Lindisfarne

KILOMETRES
MILES

+KIRKWHELPINGTON

wallington hall

NETHERWITTON

CHOLLERFORD

holy wells

RIVER SOUTH TYNE

DERE STREET

B6318

RIVER NORTH TYNE

A68

A696

devil's ca

HARTBURN

○cocklaw tower

○st oswald's chapel
and site of ✗ heavenfield

COURSE OF HADRIAN'S WALL

■BOLAM

shortflatt
tower

RIVER WANSBECK

RYAL

devil's causeway (COURSE OF ROMAN ROAD)

HEXHAM

abbey■

RIVER TYNE

A69

○port gate

A695

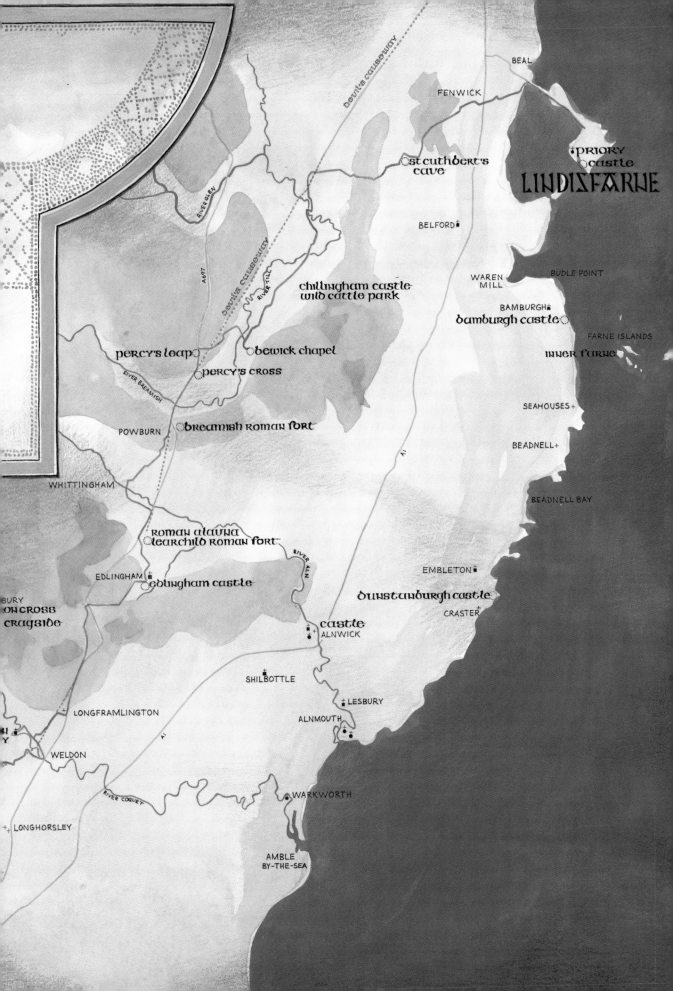

BEAL

FENWICK

st cuthbert's cave

PRIORY
castle
LINDISFARNE

BELFORD

WAREN
MILL

BUDLE POINT

chillingham castle
wild cattle park

BAMBURGH

bamburgh castle

FARNE ISLANDS

INNER FARNE

percy's leap

bewick chapel

percy's cross

SEAHOUSES+

BEADNELL+

breamish roman fort

POWBURN

BEADNELL BAY

WHITTINGHAM

roman alauna
learchild roman fort

EMBLETON

EDLINGHAM

edlingham castle

dunstanburgh castle

CRASTER+

BURY

ON CROSS

CRAGSIDE

castle
ALNWICK

SHILBOTTLE

LESBURY

LONGFRAMLINGTON

ALNMOUTH

WELDON

RIVER COQUET

WARKWORTH

LONGHORSLEY

AMBLE
BY-THE-SEA

The Priory at Hexham and its Saxon Crypt

Wilfrid built the first church at Hexham in 675-680 on such a magnificent scale that contemporaries said that no church on this side of the Alps could be compared with it. Much of the stone was robbed from the Roman town of Corstopitum. When Danish marauders attacked Hexham in 876 they completely razed the church to the ground and the site lay abandoned until the twelfth century.

A precious survival from Wilfrid's church is the Saxon crypt, one of only three in the North of England. The crypt at Hexham contained the sacred relics, particularly those of St Andrew brought from Rome by Wilfrid, and those of St Wilfrid himself. A steep and narrow stairway leads down from the present nave into the ante-chapel, where pilgrims would have been able to view the relics through a grille in the centre opening. In the roof is the Saxon ventilation shaft and in the wall one of four cresset lamps – a niche in the wall containing a bowl for holding oil which was lit to provide light. The other three lamps are in the main chapel, with two directed onto the east wall and the relics. Only the priest in charge had access to the chapel itself, probably as a precaution against the theft of the relics, which were greatly sought by common thieves or dishonest clergy during the Middle Ages.

Although of Saxon origin, the design of the crypt is enhanced by Roman stones; incorporated into the crypt are part of an altar to Apollo, a long military inscription with the partially erased name of a disgraced and murdered emperor, Geta, various mouldings and numerous examples of broached tooling.

The archbishop of York refounded the church at Hexham in 1113 as an Augustinian priory, thus ending the bleak gap of two centuries. Building was complete by about 1220, but then disaster struck again in 1296 when Scottish raiders gutted the priory and left only the walls standing. During the last rebuilding the canons abandoned the nave and restored only the eastern parts for themselves. Thus excluded from the services, the townspeople were able to worship only at St Mary's Church in the market place.

Hexham Priory, often popularly called an abbey,

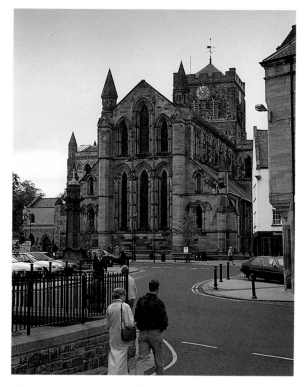

Augustinian canons rebuilt Hexham Priory in the Transitional Gothic style in 1180

became the parish church at the dissolution, and is richer in medieval furnishings than any other church in Northumberland. Surviving from the fifteenth century are a pulpit, a wonderful painted screen featuring the dance of death, choir stalls and misericords. Many Roman and Saxon sculptured fragments came to light in the Edwardian restoration which produced a new nave; the seventh-century Frith Stool is traditionally believed to have belonged to St Wilfrid himself.

THE ROUTE

Descending from the priory and the attractive market square, cross the River Tyne by the main road bridge, where beautiful parks line both banks on the upstream side. Climbing the other bank you will see nothing but a few tiny villages all the way to Lindisfarne.

The direct path onto the Devil's Causeway begins with a little lane that climbs steeply to the

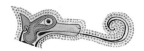

north-east from the A69 roundabout. As the gradient eases off, the lane straightens out on a raised bank between ditches, which gives it a Roman feel as it approaches Hadrian's Wall.

It is worth mentioning a detour of great historical importance: take the first lane on the left after the roundabout through Acomb and then along a farm track via Fallowfield.

The Battle of Heavenfield

There is not and never has been a settlement around the lonely chapel of St Oswald-in-Lee, which is surrounded by misty moorland just beyond Hadrian's Wall (NY 937695). The chapel commemorates an event which changed the history of Northumbria for centuries; without it the kingdom would not have been Christianised and we would not be heading for Lindisfarne.

King Oswald was a foreign invader and a Christian convert; thus the pagan King Penda of Mercia had two good reasons to hate him. Forming an alliance with King Cadwalla of Gwynedd (in North Wales), Penda advanced in AD635 with a huge British force which should have easily defeated his enemy.

The Anglian settlers formed up on the moor to await the Britons who were camped on the site of Hexham. Oswald bolstered his meagre force by erecting a make-shift wooden cross and inspiring the men with religious fervour. Against all odds, the pagans were scattered and Christian Northumbria was saved at the Battle of Heavenfield.

To thank God for his intervention, Oswald erected a permanent cross in place of the wooden one. People never forgot the importance of what happened here: the present chapel dates from 1737. W. S. Hicks gave it a comprehensive Gothic dress in 1887. Being so close to Hadrian's Wall, it comes as no surprise to find much Roman masonry, including a Roman altar decorated with scrollwork which now serves as a socket for a cross.

King Oswald fought the loathsome Penda on another occasion, but he was defeated and died a martyr. Buried at Tynemouth Priory, popular acclaim soon led to Oswald's canonisation and for over a thousand years he has been Northumberland's best-loved saint.

Although well populated in the Middle Ages, Northumberland was a lawless tract of country between Scotland and England, prey to both raiders from north of the border and to native outlaws. Redesdale to the north-west was notoriously dangerous, but nowhere was safe from attack. Each settlement needed a peel tower – a strong, square fort where people could flee and defend themselves against marauders. Cocklaw Tower near St Oswald's Chapel (NY 940712) is a peel tower which was built in the fifteenth century of strong coursed masonry. Three floors remain above ground with one room still showing its decoration. Thanks to their excellent construction, peel towers are easily recognised in the county, despite the fact that they have lain abandoned for centuries.

Hadrian's Wall

This great military construction, still the most impressive in Britain, was in answer to a co-ordinated tribal raid into the loosely garrisoned north in AD117-119. The ninth legion, which was based at York, disappeared from history in the course of some disaster about which nothing is known. The new emperor Hadrian visited the province to solve the problem of marauders and ordered a protective wall to be built. It was to be a formal frontier which would isolate the troublesome Brigantes from their allies to the north, and be a way of delaying an invasion long enough for the Roman army to prepare a decisive counter-stroke.

Agricola, one of Britain's early governors, had already built the road called the Stanegate between the forts at Corbridge (Corstopitum) and Carlisle (Luguvalium). Hadrian chose this route for the construction of the wall, which crossed the narrowest part of the island – 76 miles (122km). The wall ran a few miles north of the Stanegate, often taking advantage of a linear feature called the Whin Sill, an intrusion of hard volcanic rock which presents a steep face to the north.

A ditch defended the stone wall which was topped by a walkway, 16ft (5m) up. Behind this ran the military road, then about 150yd (46m) back was the *vallum*, a ditch and two banks forming a second line of defence. Where our path crosses the wall (NY 964692) you can see all these features

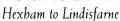

except the masonry, which was either robbed for building stone, or perhaps is now set into the foundations of the B6318 which runs between the wall and the vallum at this point.

From Hadrian's Wall to the Hart Burn

The point at which our route crosses the wall was not a Roman crossing point. The Roman highway into Scotland, Dere Street (now the A68), ran almost due north from the fort of Corstopitum on the left bank of the Tyne, passed through the Portgate, and veered west. The Devil's Causeway forked right outside the Portgate. Our path picks it up at the curiously named Click 'em in house, where the lane runs along an unmistakable Roman agger. In the many lengths where neither path nor road follows it today, the Devil's Causeway is often faintly visible in the fields if you know where to look, as for example near Ryal. But often the ditches have silted up and the agger been ploughed down. Luckily, more of the Roman road was visible in 1864 when Mr MacLauchlan surveyed it for the Duke of Northumberland, and it is his line that is marked by the Ordnance Survey.

The landscape in this area is already typical of Northumberland: bare hillsides with spread-out dairy farms. The ground is occasionally sandy, but more often peaty, boggy and covered in tufty grass with patches of damp reeds. Our footsteps follow typical Northumbrian lanes which make a right-angled turn every half mile. This is so confusing to motorists that you only ever encounter the occasional, very local, traffic.

When pilgrims came this way during the Middle Ages there were more settlements than there are today, and those remaining have clearly seen better days. Although feudal field patterns of ridge and furrow can often be seen in use as sheep runs, the deserted village is often harder to spot from the ground. At Harnham Hall (NZ 074805) there is a medieval farmhouse near a tower high up on a rocky bank. Nearby, Shortflatt Tower (NZ 078810), a peel tower, rises right by our footpath beside the How Burn.

The Devil's Causeway is faintly visible again west of this point as it passes the prehistoric menhir (NZ 065822) called Poind and His Man, a deeply grooved flat stone standing 6ft (1.8m) high on the outer bank of a broad burial tumulus. The gentry have stolen 'his man', which now graces Wallington Park.

The village of Bolam, once famous for its saddlery, has disappeared. It once had two hundred houses and a market granted by Edward I in 1305. But instead of following a route across bleak fellsides where cottages once stood, our route zig-zags through a densely planted country park with an ornamental lake. Bolam Hall itself was built in a plain classical style by John Dobson, of Newcastle railway station fame. The traces of the former village stretch over about a square mile.

The parish church of St Andrew stands on the east side of the former village in a beautiful setting with a splendid yew tree. 'Bolam' is a Viking name meaning 'the place of trees' – we still talk of the bole of a tree. Of chief architectural interest is the late Saxon tower, which was built around 960. A dowsing survey has recently revealed the plan of the church as it was at that time, including the apse at its east end. The rest of the building is Norman and Gothic. Its particular jewel is the fourteenth-century effigy of Sir Robert Reymes in the Shortflatt Chapel.

From the churchyard the footpath plunges down the steep bank to the north, although this looks an unlikely route at first, reaching the River Wansbeck at Mill Greens. A bridleway then leads into the hamlet of Hartburn, site of a Roman fortlet (NZ 087864).

We first pass the thirteenth-century church in a delightful setting on a tongue of land between the Hart Burn and another beck. The church tower may be late Saxon, although it is not as lofty as the tower of Bolam's parish church. Two daggers carved above a Maltese cross on the doorpost show that this was once a preceptory of the Knights Templar. The Early English architecture speaks of little structural change since then. In this serene building there are many carved heads and masons' marks to reward those who seek them.

The road to the Roman fortlet passes a curious folly-house, which is castellated and symmetrical with a fancy ogee window. Dr Sharpe, vicar of Hartburn from 1749 to 1792 and archdeacon of

Northumberland, built himself this delightful conceit. The fortlet site is behind the row of houses after a left bend in the road, overlooking the bridge over the Hart Burn. Roman walling appears here from time to time, but the Roman bridge is long gone. The signposted path down through a nature reserve leads to a shallow ford.

Across the Coquet
From the Hart Burn a bridleway follows the line of the Devil's Causeway closely for over a mile, and

At this shallow ford approached through a nature reserve the Roman Devil's Causeway crossed the Hart Burn

the agger is comparatively easy to see. Once in Oldpark Wood, branch left to find a bridge over the River Font.

Astride the Font is the hamlet of Netherwitton, with signs of former consequence. There is a pretty stone mill of around 1800 by the burn; but if the mill reopened there would be no dwellings to house the workers. Symptomatic of industrial de-

cline is the consciously pretty row of three gabled estate workers' cottages. Netherwitton Hall is a rectangular Queen Anne house. In cosy proximity is St Giles' Church; dating from the eighteenth century, it was sternly Gothicised in 1886.

A mile after Netherwitton we leave the lane and return to the line of the Devil's Causeway along a farm track on the right past Doe Hill Farm. Where the pylons cross, the Devil's Causeway makes its first major change of direction. Several alignments take it around the edge of the higher moors until it heads north-north-west after the Learchild fort. In the meantime a bridleway follows the line north through Todburn Moor Farm. (A detour to the east here would lead to Longhorsely on the A697, with its useful shops and a pub.) Then a lane winds down the hill in a way that is most untypical of Northumberland to rejoin the authentic line (NZ 126973) as a lane pointing straight to the site of the Roman bridge over the River Coquet. Although remains of the bridge can be seen at low water, you must either swim or make a detour to the east to cross at Weldon.

Brinkburn Priory

Medieval pilgrims probably crossed at a bridge or ford further upstream so that they could reach a comfortable night's lodging with the Augustinian canons of Brinkburn Priory. A more delightful sylvan spot would be hard to imagine. The canons came here in about 1135 and chose a small area of flood plain in a bend of the river. With woods rising steeply on all sides, the ever-present sound of rushing water imparts a deep sense of peace to the priory.

The church is complete and a splendid example of northern architecture in its transitional stage between Norman and Early English. After the dissolution of the monasteries when this priory was valued at £95, the church gradually fell into disrepair and ruin. In 1858-68 the Cadogan family saved it by employing the architect Thomas Austin to carry out a sensitive and restrained restoration. Austin and his patron recognised the original design as a masterpiece: the beautifully modelled interior gives a sense at once of both tranquillity and strength. The owners destroyed most of the other parts of the monastery in 1810 when they built the present handsome house on the site. When the last residents moved out in 1965, the then owner, Mr H. A. Cadogan Fenwick, passed the house and priory to the guardianship of the state.

From the Coquet to the Aln

If you can, it is worth making a detour a few miles up the Coquet to the village of Rothbury, where there is a famous piece of Saxon sculpture. Now forming the base of a seventeenth-century font in the parish church, a 3ft (1m) length of cross shaft has vivid and deeply carved reliefs, especially those of animals. The reliefs, dating from about 800, show the state of the world before and after mankind's fall from grace, and the ascension of Christ into heaven. There are sufficient fragments from this period in Northumbria for us to assume that each church once had its own splendid cross.

From the Coquet, Villa Lane picks up the line of the Roman road into the little village of Longframlington. The towerless church of St Mary the Virgin has a fine late twelfth-century nave and chancel arch. But the chief interest to travellers on our route lies in the facilities: two pubs, a well-stocked grocer, post office and various houses offering bed and breakfast accommodation. There is also Embleton Hall, a country house hotel. Next to the grocer is the workshop where Mr Burleigh makes Northumbrian bagpipes for native enthusiasts and exiles all over the world. You will find him always willing to give a demonstration.

From here the route gets wilder as it reaches its highest point as a stony bridleway across the bleak heather moors of Framlington Common. The line of the Devil's Causeway is uncertain from the little Edlingham Burn to the Aln.

The ancient church of St John the Baptist, Edlingham, stands in impressive isolation with its strong, squat tower facing the open moors. Most of the building, which has a rugged interior, is Norman. Nearly all of this once-important village has disappeared, but the ruined keep of the castle still stands four storeys high and is a prominent landmark. One turret leans at an acute angle, and is only prevented from falling by iron ties. Excavations have laid bare an attractive cobbled yard with

the ruins of many stone buildings lining the inside of the bailey wall.

The Learchild Roman fort once guarded the crossing of River Aln north of Edlingham. Little can be seen in the fields (NU 100115), but the place is listed in the *Ravenna Cosmography* under the name of Alauna. The Devil's Causeway starts a new alignment here as it turns around the higher ground.

Percy's Leap

Our route keeps mostly to lanes west of the main road as far as the River Breamish. The first port of call is Whittingham, a pretty hamlet spread out along the wide grassy banks of the River Aln. At the church of St Bartholomew there is a well-built Saxon tower, probably dating from *c*737. Across the stream is the former castle – in 1845 Lady Ravensworth rebuilt it as an almshouse, adding romantic battlements and machiolations, but this lovely structure is now abandoned. Here you will find a pub, a post office and village shop.

The Norman church of the Holy Trinity at Old Bewick enjoys an isolated hillside site with wide views to Scotland

Glanton is a pleasant stone village, stretching along a broad turnpike road, with fine views of the Breamish and Aln valleys. Here in 1648 Colonel Sanderson captured 150 sleeping Royalist troopers. There is a bird research station with many exhibits.

Before the high lane descends down to the hamlet of Powburn you can see Crawley Farm on a prominent spur. This marks the site of the Breamish Roman fort (NU 068166) which guarded the crossing of the River Breamish. Its outline can still be seen as a rectangular bank 328 × 164ft (100 × 50m) surrounded by a ditch, but the masonry was robbed in about 1300 for building the Crawley Tower.

Here the route rejoins the line of the Devil's Causeway. Although shared for 2 miles (3km) with the main road, it does pass the historic site of the

Battle of Hedgeley Moor (1464), part of the sordid dynastic struggle romantically known to posterity as the Wars of the Roses. The splendid Percy's Cross stands in a farmyard (NU 054194), its shaft ornamented by fishes and crescents. According to tradition, it marks the spot to which the wounded Sir Ralph Percy, third son of the Duke of Northumberland, crawled and expired after the battle. He had already changed sides four times – on this occasion he had fought with the losing Lancastrian army. A little way up the road, a notice draws attention to a walled copse called Percy's Leap. Here the duke had leapt between the two stone markers and wounded his horse.

Wild Cattle
We leave the A697 at a sawmill immediately after this and make our way to the isolated chapel of the Holy Trinity, Old Bewick, up a lane (NU 067222). This former Norman ruin was extensively restored in 1867. It has a memorable position, with wide views to the distant Cheviot Hills in the north-west.

About 2 miles (3km) to the north is the famous herd of wild white cattle in the landscaped park at Chillingham Castle. From the shape of their skulls they are known to be descended from the original British wild ox. So wild are they that any human help in rearing a calf will result in rejection by the mother because of the human smell left on her offspring. You will need advice to locate the whereabouts of the cattle in the park. As a result of the outbreak of foot and mouth disease in the 1960s another herd has been started at a secret location. The church and castle are well worth a visit.

St Cuthbert's Cave
From Chillingham Castle you can either make your way back to the Devil's Causeway via Chatton and Fowberry Tower, but then leave it at East Horton, or take a more direct line to Old Hazelrigg (NU 057331). In either case the objective is St Cuthbert's traditional place of retreat, a splendid long cave under a sandstone bluff, deep in a wood in the Kyloe Hills. It is well sheltered from the east winds by Cockenheugh Rigg and looks onto a beautiful glade. Here Cuthbert came to avoid the distractions of monastic life on Lindis-

farne and tradition also says that his body rested in the cave when the monks were fleeing with their most precious relics from the marauding Danes.

Journey's End
From St Cuthbert's Cave a footpath leads through the plantations on Buckton Moor. Suddenly the coast appears and we pass through the settlement of Fenwick onto the tidal wetlands along the shore, a national nature reserve which includes Holy Island itself. The illustration on p89 shows Lindisfarne from this point of view. The shortest crossing, from Beal Sands to Chare Ends, follows the line of tall posts across the sands. This is the original line that was followed by medieval pilgrims and we owe its recent restoration to a government employment scheme. Do make sure that the tide will not catch you in the middle. If in doubt, consult the tide tables at the mainland end of the causeway.

The Life and Shrine of St Cuthbert
Cuthbert was a shepherd boy from the Lammermuir Hills in the Scottish Lowlands. In 651, at the age of about sixteen, he entered the Celtic monastery of Melrose. The Venerable Bede's *Life of Cuthbert* tells us that he was robust and strong, doing everything with energetic zeal throughout his life. His pleasant affability brought him the duties of guestmaster at Ripon monastery, a foundation of Melrose; later in life he was prior of Melrose and prior of Lindisfarne. But wherever he served his speciality was to go on long missionary journeys for up to a month at a time, preaching in remote villages and farmsteads in the hills – to Cuthbert the soul of a peasant was just as important as that of a king.

Returning to Lindisfarne after these journeys, Cuthbert would retire to the solitude of a hermitage on the bare slab of rock in the sea near the priory which still bears the name St Cuthbert's Isle. As time went by these periods of secluded meditation grew more important. In 676, as a result of his 'long and spotless active life', Cuthbert was allowed by his abbot and monks the special privilege of retiring to 'the stillness of divine contemplation' on the Farne Islands. Bede also supplies precious details of his humble cabin and the vegetable patch there which sustained the hermit.

Eleven years after Cuthbert's burial at Lindisfarne, the monks elevated his body to a new shrine and discovered its incorruption: the saint appeared to be asleep. From that time onward it was an object of special veneration. Cuthbert's cult was already well established by the end of the seventh century and he had remained Northumbria's favourite saint.

Cuthbert's body, its shrine and the famous Lindisfarne Gospels began a long journey for a new home when the Vikings threatened Lindisfarne in 875. The monks and their most precious relics rested at St Cuthbert's Cave, Derwentmouth, on the Cumbrian coast, at Ripon and, for a century, at Chester-le-Street. Only in 995 did they find a permanent home at Durham, where a Saxon church was specially built for them and consecrated four years later. When the monks translated the remains into the magnificent Norman cathedral in 1104, they again verified the miraculous incorruption. Henry VIII's men destroyed the shrine at the Reformation but the body was either buried at the same site, now marked by an inscribed stone, or at a secret site nearby known only to three Benedictine brothers – this knowledge is passed on to three brothers of the next generation.

The green lane below Cockenheugh Rigg which leads to St Cuthbert's Cave in a wooded glade up the hill

On Lindisfarne the site of Cuthbert's original tomb became a shrine again in 1122 when the monastery was rebuilt as a Benedictine daughter of Durham Cathedral priory. The site can be seen today within the grassy apse of the Norman church: the area behind the main altar was the most sacred place for burial throughout the Middle Ages. The passage through the presbytery wall may well have been provided to give pilgrims access to the tomb without their having to pass through the choir which was reserved for the brethren.

Cuthbert's portable altar of wood, his fine jewelled pectoral cross and his wooden coffin can all be seen in the fascinating museum of the Northumbrian church in Durham Cathedral.

The Celtic Monastery on Lindisfarne

The story of Holy Island begins in 634 with the mission of Aidan. Aidan's first act was to ask for Christian teachers from St Columba's famous monastery of Iona to spread the gospel throughout Northumbria. This first mission failed, but Aidan

Viking raiders destroy St Cuthbert's Abbey on Lindisfarne in AD875

himself took the Christian message to Northumbria, having chosen Lindisfarne as his base.

Aidan may have been attracted to Lindisfarne because of its resemblance to his beloved Iona and its position close to the royal stronghold at Bamburgh. The name Lindisfarne is Celtic, meaning 'the land by the Lindis', a small stream now called the Low which appears only at low water.

The monks built the early monastery in the Celtic style: simple and austere. It probably consisted of a number of small huts or cells made of wattle and daub and timber. The roof thatch might have been held down with diagonal tethering ropes and 'tent pegs'. The whole enclosure would have been surrounded by a low earth bank. Within this enclosure were also the church, a communal refectory and kitchen, a dormitory for brethren and perhaps another for novices, an infirmary and a guest-house. There was probably also a workshop area.

Outside the monastic enclosure was probably an Anglian village, as well as arable fields and the stock enclosures. Nothing remains of the early monastery; its exact location is unknown, but a plausible position for the monastic enclosure would be in the area of the present village and priory. Probably only the church had two storeys, with a nave and aisles of typical basilican form. All other buildings would have been low and rectangular except for the group of tiny circular cells.

The Lindisfarne monastery was entirely destroyed by Viking raids in 875 and it was not reoccupied until it was refounded in about 1090 under a different rule – as a dependency of the Benedictine order at Durham Cathedral priory.

From their religious centre Aidan and his fifteen successors as bishops of Lindisfarne evangelised the whole of Northumbria. The monastery was an important centre of learning at a time when conditions were extremely difficult in Europe.

The finest surviving work of art produced by the monks must be the exquisite Lindisfarne Gospels which are kept in the British Library. Apart from small decorated initials most of the pages are plain script, with the wonderful Celtic ornament confined to the start of each gospel. The gospels remained at Lindisfarne until the monks fled in 875. Tradition says that the book was miraculously saved when the monks attempted to cross to Ireland.

Another famous treasure of the Celtic monastery is the Stonyhurst Gospel of St John, a sixth-century manuscript which the canons of Durham found when they opened St Cuthbert's wooden coffin in 1104. The leather covering has beautiful Celtic ornament. Less well known in England is the Codex Amiatinus, a vast bible made at Lindisfarne in the late seventh century and intended as a gift for the pope. Its bearer died in Tuscany and it is now in the state archives in Florence. So large is it that two bearers are needed to bring it to a reader's table!

In the priory museum on the island you can see many carved stones and other finds connected with both the Celtic monastery and the Benedictine priory.

THE PATH TO HOLY ISLAND:
HEXHAM TO LINDISFARNE

ROUTE LENGTH: 59½ miles (96km)   MAPS: OS 1:50,000 Nos 75, 81, 87

PUBLIC HOUSES

Map ref	Name of Pub	Location
NY 935639	County Hotel**#	Priestpopple, Hexham
NY 934643	Globe**	Battle Hill, Hexham
NY 987686	Errington Arms**	Portgate on Hadrian's Wall, 2 miles (3km) E of path
NZ 143967	Linden Hall Hotel***#	Longhorsely, 2 miles (3km) E of path
NU 132010	Granby***#	Longframlington
NU 132010	Anglers' Arms**	Longframlington
NU 125420	Crown & Anchor**	Lindisfarne
NU 180350	Lord Crew Arms**#	Bamburgh, near end of path

Key: *** Highly recommended by the *Good Pub Guide*   * Recommended
     ** Recommended by the *Good Pub Guide*   #Accommodation

BED & BREAKFAST ACCOMMODATION

Map ref	Name of House	Location/Telephone number
NU 055017	Orchard House	High Street, Rothbury, 3 miles (5km) W of path. Tel: (0669) 20684
NU 098062	New Moor House	A697/B6341 near Edlingham. Tel: (0665) 74638

ISOLATED PUBLIC TELEPHONES

Map ref	Location of Telephone
NY 953657	Oakwood
NZ 016743	Ryal crossroads
NZ 019775	Kirkheaton, 500yd (1km) W of path
NZ 084816	Bolam Low House on edge of country park
NZ 088861	Hartburn
NU 112090	Edlingham
NU 028308	East Horton (path leaves Devil's Causeway)
NU 042362	Holburn, 1 mile (2km) W of path

VILLAGES OR HAMLETS WITH GENERAL STORES

After Hexham there are no shops until Netherwitton 14 miles (23km); then Longhorsely 2 miles (3km) E of path, Longframlington, Whittingham, Glanton, Powburn, Chillingham, Chatton, Fenwick, Lindisfarne.

TOURIST INFORMATION OFFICES

Hexham, Corbridge, Morpeth, Rothbury, Alnwick, Wooler, Lindisfarne.

7

THE PILGRIMS' WAY

his walk has two faces. It can be seen as a pilgrimage like others in the book, calling at historic places related to its theme, and seeking out, like Hilaire Belloc a century ago, the old road from Winchester to Canterbury. Or, thanks to the Countryside Commission and the Ramblers' Association, it can be followed as a nature ramble along the more remote course taken by the North Downs Way long-distance footpath. In this case the path only begins at Farnham. The Pilgrims' Way and the North Downs Way are parallel, and in general pilgrims follow the foot of the downs while the ramblers pursue their course higher up the slopes. Sometimes the two paths coincide and at others the historic route is uncertain.

The Prehistoric Ridgeway

This book has stressed the prehistoric importance of the numerous ridgeways which converge at Salisbury Plain. The most vital of all was the Harroway (Hoar or Hard Way) along the Cretaceous chalk ridge of the North Downs from Dover to Stonehenge, for this was the main route for all Britain's immigrants from the continent of Europe – the Dover Straits was still a land bridge until about 5000BC.

The ridge was a trackway but not a densely settled area in ancient times. It does, however, yield much evidence of life in those distant days: the skull of Swanscombe man found near Gravesend dates back 300,000 years, while the mesolithic (middle Stone Age) site at Abinger is the oldest dwelling site in Britain. The neolithic burial chamber by the Medway called Kit's Coty House and the Bronze Age urn cemetery near Farnham are just two more instances of the unfolding story, as are the Titsey Roman temple, villa and pottery.

Local variations do occur to alter the character of the landscape in places. This is particularly obvious towards the west end of the North Downs in Surrey, where the chalk strata are thin and the underlying greensand is thick. The so-called greensand is not a sand and is rarely green, but it is a sandstone associated with sandy soil. On these heaths pine trees and heather flourish and the track is often called Sandy Lane. In Surrey the Pilgrims' Way passes between the two rock types. At Puttenham, for example, the Way crosses the boundary and so both chalk and sandstone may be found in the buildings of the village.

Once into Kent the Pilgrims' Way keeps to the chalk, but often by only a few yards. In this way it remains on well-drained rock but does not undulate so much. The North Downs Way, on the other hand, tends to stay well up the chalk scarp and enjoy wider views. At Chilham both paths turn sharply left and cut back right through the ridge to reach Canterbury on the boundary between the chalk and the London clay.

The yew is the characteristic tree along the Pilgrims' Way and often the route is marked by a line of them. On the greensand the Scots pine is the dominant tree. Most of the native trees grow naturally along the way – for example, oak, sycamore, hawthorn, elder, ash and field maple. Among the wild flowers are the Canterbury bell, hawkweed, scabia, campion, dog rose, mallow and meadowsweet. Nettles are often copious where the path narrows, and it is therefore inadvisable to wear shorts. In the autumn wild mushrooms are a wonderful sight in the woods.

The first leg of the Pilgrims' Way, from Winchester to the Harroway and the North Downs at Farnham, does not offer such good walking as the stretches in Surrey and Kent. Given the choice, some travellers may prefer to visit the historic sites by bicycle and then continue on foot from Farnham. In fact, it is possible and highly enjoyable to bicycle all the way to Canterbury along a series of delightful and varied country lanes – that is the beauty of having the two parallel routes.

THE PILGRIMS' WAY
Winchester to Canterbury

Near the end of the Pilgrims' Way lies Chilham, valued by many visitors as a perfect English village

The Life and Cult of Thomas Becket
Festival of the Martyrdom: 29 December
Translation of the Relics: 7 July

Several rivers penetrate through gaps in the North Downs and impede travel: the Itchen, the Wey, the Mole, the Darent, the Medway and the Great Stour. Each had a prehistoric ford and medieval pilgrims would have used some of these, but more often they would have crossed by ferry (the Mole and the Medway) or walked over one of the bridges built by monks or some philanthropist. The River Medway was always the greatest barrier. Today the North Downs Way makes a monstrous detour all the way down to Rochester and crosses on, of all things, a motorway bridge. To the historically minded it seems nothing short of criminal that the Countryside Commission ignored the old road, now a quiet lane, down to Snodland and the site of the medieval ferry. The commissioners could have built a footbridge to connect with the old causeway to Burham on the other side and so back onto the North Downs. This way would be both pretty and direct.

Reliable details of the lives of saints who are venerated at holy shrines are all too often few and far between. However, this deficiency of information does not apply to St Thomas Becket – there are thirty narratives of his death, some of them written by eye witnesses, and a dozen biographies appeared within ten years of his martyrdom.

Thomas Becket was born in about 1118 into a prosperous family at Cheapside in the City of London. After a good education, first at Merton Priory, then later in London and Paris, he entered business. Soon he appeared in the retinue of Theobald, then Archbishop of Canterbury, went to Rome, and studied canon law at Bologna. He was tall, handsome, learned and very able, so that in 1155 Henry II made him Chancellor of England.

Thomas and King Henry were close friends and men of the world, who joked, hunted, feasted, debated and reformed the kingdom after the chaos

Pilgrims'

Winchester

king's worthy · itchen stoke · bishop's sutton · ropley dean · ropley · alton · chawton · farringdon · holybourne · bentley · far...

headbourne worthy · martyr worthy · east tisted · river wey

Legend
- 🏛 medieval cathedral
- ⛪ (arch)bishop's palace
- ✟ important medieval church
- ⛪ anchorite's cell
- 🏠 pilgrim's hospice
- 🏚 ancient roadside inn
- ⛰ neolithic tomb

north downs

tatsfield · chevening · otford · cuxton · black boy inn · burl... · old ferry · snodland · bull · ayle...

titsey · hogtrough hill · westerham · kemsing · st clere · wrotham · trottiscliffe · river darent · river medway

sevenoaks

ma...

seale   puttenham   guildford   st martha   ranmore common   ford   box hill   gatton   merstham

old ferry   st catherine's   compton   albury   shere   gomshall   wotton   westcott heath   dorking   reigate

river wey   river mole

kilometres

miles

ay Winchester to Canterbury

boxley abbey   detling chapel   north downs   harrietsham   lenham   charing   challoch lees   boughton   chilham   river great stour   Canterbury

of Stephen's reign. Thomas enjoyed a lavish life-style and commanded immense public expenditure. He raised this money by increasing taxes, particularly on the Church. But within this courtly splendour he led an inner life of chastity and austerity that was hidden from most men's eyes. The king misunderstood his friend, for when he persuaded him to accept the vacant see of Canterbury – which Thomas did reluctantly – he expected Thomas' active help in all his schemes, and particularly in submitting the clergy to secular courts. Thus were laid the foundations of the famous quarrel which had such far-reaching consequences.

During the Middle Ages, anyone who could read, whether he was an ordained priest or not, could plead 'benefit of clergy' and if accused of a crime could be tried by the ecclesiastical courts without reference to the king and his laws. King Henry wanted clergy convicted by the Church to be handed over to his courts; he also wanted a formal say in the election of bishops. When the new archbishop resolved to retain the Church's privileges and refused to give his consent to the king's wishes, he was insulted and mocked at court.

The strain made Becket ill and on 2 November 1164, two years after his election as Archbishop of Canterbury, he fled the country into exile, after which Henry banished Becket's friends, relatives and servants. In England many of the bishops were dismayed by the archbishop's unwillingness to appease the king.

The archbishop rallied the king of France to his cause and also the pope who threatened to excommunicate the king of England. As a result of such a severe threat, a reconciliation was arranged during a meeting of the protagonists in France. After six years in exile, Thomas resumed his position as archbishop in December 1170 amid remarkable scenes of popular rejoicing.

But Thomas had lost none of his resolve. At Bayeux the king's courtiers whipped the impatient Henry into such a towering rage that he uttered the fateful curse: 'What cowards have I about me, that none will rid me from this turbulent low-born priest?'. Four knights who heard these bitter words, Fitzurse, de Morville, de Tracy and le Breton, left by separate routes for England and a rendezvous at Saltwood Castle near Canterbury.

Meanwhile, Thomas was aware of his approaching death. On Christmas Day in the cathedral he ritually cursed the Church's enemies, extinguishing a candle and throwing it to the ground as he pronounced each name. On 29 December the four knights, plus de Broc, usurper of Saltwood Castle, delivered an ultimatum in which Becket was summoned to the royal court to answer for his misconduct. After a violent argument, the unarmed knights withdrew, girded on their swords and attempted to force an entry into the archbishop's chamber. Terrified monks pleaded and dragged the willing martyr into the sanctuary of the church.

At about five o'clock the murderers burst into the cathedral, though were momentarily overawed by the solemn gloom. Recovering, they advanced into the transept but were again halted, this time by the archbishop's majestic appearance in full clerical dress. In vain they called on him to surrender. They tried to drag him out of the sanctuary but the powerful Becket and his faithful monk, Brother Grim, hung on. The bloody attack began, succeeding blows forcing the archbishop to his knees. When he lay dead one of the murderers gratuitously crushed his skull and scattered the brains across the cold stone floor.

Before Becket's martyrdom, Canterbury's most important shrine had been that of St Alphege, who had been martyred by marauding Danes. What, then, made the shrine of St Thomas Becket the most famous and popular in Christendom? Consider what the zealous knights had done, for every circumstance combined to impress upon the popular mind the ghastly horror of their deed. They had murdered a priest in a sanctuary. He was the head of the country's clergy and the sanctuary was the principal church in the land. He had died in God's name defending his Church's rights and had often openly proclaimed his willingness to die in this cause. When confronted by armed attackers he had refused to flee or hide, but had behaved with supreme courage and dignity.

Soon after Becket's death miracles began to occur – so many in fact, that within the year a papal legation arrived to test the authenticity of the

stories: formal canonisation of the martyr took place on Ash Wednesday 1173. The people flocked to the shrine, the cult receiving a tremendous boost from the translation of the relics in July 1174.

The king found himself in deep trouble: he was fighting against his son in Normandy and was powerless to prevent the depredations in the North of William the Lion, king of the Scots. Realising the significant effect an act of penance might have on the imagination of his people, he decided to go on a pilgrimage himself, travelling from Normandy via Winchester and the Pilgrims' Way.

As the royal pilgrim entered the city, barefoot and wearing a hair-shirt, the crowds noticed that blood streamed from his feet. Falling to his knees at the martyr's tomb in the crypt Henry prayed for a long time, sobbing, groaning and weeping bitterly. Then he restored the Church's privileges, granted

The double transepts and tower of Canterbury Cathedral

40 marks yearly for candles at the shrine and submitted himself to a public scourging: bowing his head into the tomb the king received five strokes from each bishop and abbot, then three from each of the eighty monks. Exhausted and broken in body and spirit he kept a night-long vigil at Becket's shrine on the cold stones. Humbled, defeated and penitent, he returned to London the next day.

Historic Reminders of the Pilgrims
Not only is the shrine of St Thomas the most holy in Britain, but the pilgrimage to visit it is and was the most famous and popular: it is, indeed, The Pilgrims' Way. As such it is a must for inclusion here, but it is so famous that many books deal with the pilgrimage from Winchester to Canterbury and

nothing else. Thus it is appropriate to treat this pilgrimage in less detail than the rest, mentioning only briefly each of the historic features along the route.

Why Winchester?

The reason that we shall begin our journey from Winchester when Chaucer's pilgrims set out from the Tabard Inn at Southwark, is that no one today would want to risk his life walking from London to Canterbury along the busy and dangerous A2. I once did it on a bicycle, but would not do so again.

Hilaire Belloc provides us with a more detailed explanation. From Cherbourg to Southampton is the safest way across the Channel, for a sailor is only briefly out of sight of the Barfleur Hills on the

end of the Cherbourg peninsula, or of St Catherine's Hill on the southern tip of the Isle of Wight. Furthermore, the shoreline means that his chances of escape from a gale or adverse tide are good in either direction, especially on the English side where there are entrances to Southampton Water whether he is blown east or west. From earliest times man has favoured this wonderful anchorage, with all the ridgeways to different parts of Britain close at hand.

As Canterbury is the focus for traffic from all the ports of Kent, so Winchester became the focus for trade and travellers through Southampton, and by late Saxon times it had become the capital of England. The Normans, too, favoured Winchester, which continued as a more important base for the court than London was, until about 1250. Winchester Cathedral bears historical evidence of this fact; the longest church in Norman England, it remains so to the present day.

The Waynflete chantry chapel in Winchester Cathedral, which was built in the Perpendicular Gothic style. Bishop Waynflete died in 1486

Quite apart from its strategic and political importance, twelfth-century Winchester had famous schools of carving and illumination, plus the shrine of St Swithun, its ninth-century bishop; long before the murder of Thomas Becket, St Swithun's shrine was a popular place of pilgrimage. So when Becket, the holy blissful martyr, drew the faithful to Canterbury from all over Europe, a large number came through Winchester and there joined the Englishmen travelling up from the Westcountry.

The First Stage: Winchester to Farnham

Leaving the glories of medieval Winchester behind, the first relic we find is at Headbourne Worthy, the most important of all four Worthies at the time of the Domesday survey. St Swithun's Church is entirely Saxon and above its original west door is a Saxon rood, a relief carving of international value: the three over-life-size figures depict Christ, the Virgin Mary and St John, with the hand of God reaching down from a cloud. Even though they were defaced by Puritan zeal, they remain impressive.

King's Worthy, Martyr Worthy, Itchen Stoke and New Alresford, although pretty villages along the River Itchen, preserve nothing relevant to our theme. At Bishop's Sutton, however, are the remains of a possible anchorite's cell attached to the north side of St Nicholas' Church: here a revered hermit lived who was able to participate in the Mass through a sighting hole called a 'hagioscope', benefiting from the alms of passing pilgrims and in turn offering them advice and comfort.

At Ropley Dean on the Alresford to Alton road is an ancient roadside inn, the Anchor, which was once used by pilgrims. Then, after the watershed that takes the old road into the Wey Valley, and a mile beyond East Tisted, we find a former hospice, called on old maps Pilgrims' (now Pelham) Place; often along the Pilgrims' Way, buildings are called Pilgrims' House or Pilgrims' Cottage, but sometimes it is because they lie on the road and not because they are former hospices.

The Way continues through Farringdon and Chawton (Jane Austen's house) to the handsome little town of Alton, then along the modern highway via Holybourne, Froyle (where pilgrims would have feared the dangerous outlaws in Alice Holt) and Bentley into Farnham and Surrey.

Farnham was an important stage of the pilgrims' route: the Norman castle was a palace of the bishops of Winchester. Another pilgrims' hospice survives here as the Old Vicarage in Church Lane. Other pilgrims would have sought shelter at nearby Waverley Abbey, the Cistercians' first monastery in England.

The Second Stage: Farnham to Dorking

From a fork called Whiteway End (SU 877476) on the road to the Hog's Back ridge, the Pilgrims' Way assumes its special character of always following the southern flank of the hills. At Seale the church of St Lawrence on a little mound owes its very existence to the pilgrimage, having been built early in the thirteenth century by the abbots of Waverley. At Puttenham there was a pilgrims' market in the churchyard, strategically timed to distract the faithful on their way to the Feast of the Translation. Whether it is old or not, the name of the pub, the Good Intent, certainly suits the Pilgrims' Way.

At Compton, St Nicholas' Church is a fascinating building along the old road. The square Saxon tower dates from the tenth century. The Normans built a conventional chevronned chancel arch and beyond that a two-storeyed sanctuary. The congregation sees one altar framed by a second Norman arch and, directly above it, a second altar beyond a hoary oak railing. There is no sure explanation for this unique arrangement, but the upper sanctuary may have contained a valuable relic. The church has a second anchorite's cell: originally the hermit would have looked through the window in the north chancel wall which was aligned with the Saxon altar, but later rebuilding moved his or her cell to the south side where a quatrefoil window looks onto the Norman altar. Standing near the church on the lane through the village is a well-loved, half-timbered house called White Hart Cottage: local tradition says that it was a pilgrims' hospice.

Shortly after Compton, the Way offers a charming view of Loseley House, famed for its dairy products, especially the ice-cream which is of a

The eighteenth-century City Mill on the River Itchen once belonged to the Priory of Wherwell – now it is an unusual youth hostel in the centre of Winchester

quality rarely found in England today. Architecturally, it is the finest Elizabethan mansion in Surrey, now known to be an enlargement of a medieval hall, and open to the public every season.

Before crossing the River Wey, the picturesque ruins of St Catherine's pilgrims' chapel may be seen standing on a prominent knoll overlooking the river. The chapel dates from 1317 and was originally highly ornamental, like a large sandstone casket: the huge buttresses, for example, once sported boastful Gothic pinnacles. The fact that it housed another precious relic best explains the peculiarities of the building, which include no less than five doors.

A little lane descends past ancient cottages to the medieval crossing; once called Pilgrims' Ferry, it has now been replaced by a footbridge. Some pilgrims would have gone a mile downstream into Guildford, an important market town where the

chief fair occurred at Christmas to cater for the faithful who were travelling to the original Feast of the Martyrdom. Surviving from those days are four medieval churches and the huge motte of the Norman castle, strengthened by, among others, Henry II during the course of his civil wars. The oldest inn is the Angel Hotel where the thirteenth-century cellars are now a bar; other pilgrims would have resorted to Friary Street and the Dominicans' hospitality.

Shalford lies on the east side of the Pilgrims' Ferry. Its great fair, called Becket's Fair, grew to cover 140 acres (57ha) and lasted for seven days, starting on 15 August to catch the pilgrims returning from the Feast of the Translation. Local tradition says that the festival provided John Bunyan with the model for Vanity Fair in *The Pilgrim's Progress*, and that the nearby marshes of the Wey were the original Slough of Despond in that book. As Bunyan lived for a while in a cottage called Horn Hatch facing Shalford Green, it is conceivable that the presence of the Pilgrims' Way inspired the entire allegory. Shalford derives its name from the ancient word meaning 'shallow ford', which was swept away for the Wey Navigation.

The sandy course of the old road now makes a rare climb, through woods called The Chantries, to a hilltop that commands magnificent views: St Martha's Chapel, rebuilt from ruins in 1848 using the old materials, perfectly expresses the lonely spirit of this exposed site far above the village of Chilworth (and its extensive Georgian gunpowder factory) – it is not surprising that Martha's Hill is believed to be Bunyan's model for the Hill Difficulty and that pagan rituals took place here.

Albury Church – the long-disused church in Albury Park – is believed to be the most ancient in Surrey: certainly it now has a romantic air and about half of its walls are Saxon. In 1840 the squire, Henry Drummond, was responsible for having the entire village moved from where it was spoiling the view from his house, to a new site outside the park.

Crossing the Tilling Bourne at Chantry Ford, the Pilgrims' Way enters the famous village of Shere, where the picturesqueness owes more to Victorian contrivance than to fortunate accident. Nevertheless, parts of the White Horse Inn date back to the fourteenth century. Among the exquisite Early English stonework in St James' Church, look for the quatrefoil window and hagioscope in the chancel's north wall, modifications which allowed Christine, the anchoress of Shere, to receive the sacrament and to see the altar from her sunless cell. Pilgrims and parishioners gave food to the anchoress through a grating on the churchyard side.

Gomshall boasts an ancient roadside inn called the Black Horse; then the old road crosses the mouth of Coldkitchen Combe to reach its usual terrace at the foot of Hackhurst Down. The Ordnance Survey formerly took the Pilgrims' Way along the top of Ranmore Common and, although this was because the Way was confused with a later

White Hart Cottage at Compton in Surrey is by tradition a former pilgrims' hospice (Photo: author)

drove road, the path along a huge glade on top of the Weald is now a better way for walkers to reach the Mole crossing. The Victorians' most successful architect, Sir George Gilbert Scott, built the Gothic church up there for the Victorians' most prosperous builder, Thomas Cubitt.

The Third Stage: Dorking to Otford

The Mole is best crossed with the North Downs Way on the stepping-stones (TQ 172513) at the ancient Giles Green ford, or at the footbridge 220yd (200m) downstream. There is another old roadside inn south of Burford Bridge on the right bank. Regaining the chalk at Box Hill, lovers of Bunyan will recognise the actual place-name Doubting Castle.

In Reigate, a mile south of the Downs, a pilgrim chapel of St Thomas and an Augustinian priory once stood. Gatton, a much derided rotten borough, is the first of four park enclosures which have been permitted to abolish the ancient right of way (the others are all in Kent, at Titsey, Chevening and Chilham). The little fifteenth-century pilgrims' church in Gatton Park was totally transformed in the 1830s into a Gothic confection decorated with baubles, at the instigation of Lord Monson after he had returned from the Grand Tour.

St Katharine's, Merstham, is a noble thirteenth-century church sited out of the village on the Pilgrims' Way at a spot where an easy pass comes through the Downs. Frescoes depicting the life of St Thomas originally decorated the south wall.

Before Titsey the Way passes a spring called St Thomas' Well, and then comes another diversion of the old road around the enclosed Titsey Park. Near St James' Church is Pilgrims' Lodge, an old hospice. As at Albury, a Victorian church stands on a new site outside the park.

At the end of Tatsfield parish the Pilgrims' Way enters Kent and soon comes upon another former hospice called Pilgrim House, which can be found a short distance up the scarp near Hogtrough Hill (TQ 449564). After the next diversion around Chevening Park (where high security makes it particularly inadvisable to trespass along the old road), the old church by its east gates repays a visit. Originally dedicated to St Botolph, patron saint of

travellers, the church was once a shrine along the Way; now it is more notable for the memorials to the Stanhope family, who suppressed the right of way through their park in 1792.

The Pilgrims' Way now approaches the River Darent and, as before, it leads from one spur of the Downs to another across an old ford. The bridge at Otford may have been maintained by the archbishops of Canterbury, for they had a palace here from the twelfth century. The manor became a place of shelter with special sanctity for pilgrims because it had been a favourite residence of the martyred Thomas Becket – the water supply, now in private grounds to the east, was called Becket's Well. Archbishop Warham rebuilt the palace on a magnificent scale in 1503-18 around a courtyard 240ft (73m) across, and on several occasions he was host to Henry VIII. What remains is a complete corner tower plus one-eighth of the rest, which has been picturesquely converted into cottages behind St Bartholomew's Church. Some of the palace's fittings, oak panelling and chimney-pieces are said to have been used in the Bull Inn.

The Fourth Stage:
Otford to the River Medway

In the Middle Ages the Pilgrims' Way from Otford was a very busy highway. Travellers would have joined it at several places in Surrey, but from then on the main road from London along the Darent Valley increased its importance, especially when invasion threatened from the Kent coast. Why Archbishop Warham rebuilt Otford is a mystery, for the archbishops already owned the vast palace at Knole 3 miles (5km) away, as well as another one at Wrotham, less than a day's journey along the Pilgrims' Way after the village of Kemsing (where there was a minor shrine to St Edith). Here the archbishops had been granted the manor in the tenth century. The palace was never as popular as Otford and in the fourteenth century Archbishop Simon Islip demolished Wrotham for its materials, which were used to build a new palace at Maidstone. The slight ruins lie east of the splendid church of St George, known for its unique arch under the tower: as the tower abutted the edge of the consecrated ground, this was the only way left

The Carmelite Fathers once again welcome pilgrims to the hospice at Aylesford Priory (Photo: author)

to form a processional route around the outside of the building.

Medieval pilgrims would have been able to seek shelter at two nearby hospices. The first, still known as Pilgrim House but now unsympathetically modernised, is north-north-west of Trotterscliffe (TQ 636609) and was marked as the Kentish Drover by the Victorian Ordnance Survey. The second lay on the spur to the Medway ferry at Crookhorn Wood (TQ 670632), where both a hospice and the Black Boy Inn stood at a crossroads now called Holly Hill.

The crossing of the River Medway is now a serious problem. Clearly, the medieval pilgrims would have gone down from the Crookhorn Wood ridge straight into Snodland, where the village High Street leads past some ancient cottages to the old ferry. On the left bank is Snodland's All Saints Church with the echoing tower of Burham Old Church aligned along a causeway across the marshes on the opposite side. It is the shortest route between the good chalk of the Downs; it is also the prettiest, which only makes it more deplorable that public time and money have been wasted in the acquisition of new rights of way all the way to a motorway bridge and back, instead of building a footbridge at the historic crossing.

There is another historic crossing of great interest upstream at Aylesford, the limit of the tides (unfortunately, the approach for walkers is now through an unattractive suburban and industrial sprawl). This may have been a prehistoric ford. Here in 1170, the very year of Becket's martyrdom, the de Grey family established a pilgrims' hospice; the pilgrims' hall survives from that date and is the finest example in England. The pilgrims would have eaten as well as slept in the hall. In 1242 the crusader, Baron Richard de Grey, fled the Holy Land as the Saracens took the last Christian strongholds, and brought back on his ship a group of monks who had been displaced from Mount Carmel. He gave them the hospice and some land to establish the first Carmelite priory in England, which was honoured in 1247 by an international meeting of the order. The monks built the lovely fourteenth-century bridge over the Medway and a large priory, which was dissolved by Henry VIII. After its being used for centuries as a private house, the Carmelites repurchased the site, initially out of historic interest, but happily in 1949 the Carmelite fathers returned here and have built a fine retreat, a shrine (to St Simon Stock) and a guest-house for one hundred pilgrims. The ancient hall is still in use as a refectory.

The Fifth Stage: the River Medway to Canterbury

Now modern pilgrims are on the last leg of their journey with only one more river to cross, and that at the gates of Canterbury. The medieval Pilgrims' Way led from the Medway ferry past an ancient roadside inn at Bull Lane, Eccles, to the south of Burham. Nearby (TQ 744608) is the best-known prehistoric monument on the ridgeway, a neolithic burial chamber called Kit's Coty House. Three upright megaliths support a massive capstone, but the 200ft (60m) long barrow which once covered it has been completely destroyed by erosion and ploughing. Little Kit's Coty House is a jumbled group of about twenty sarsen stones to the south, the remains of another barrow that was wrecked three hundred years ago.

Medieval pilgrims at this stage would have headed for Boxley Abbey, not just for its hospitality, but because the famous Holy Rood of Grace was probably the most precious relic at any shrine along the Pilgrims' Way. The wooden image on the crucifix miraculously rolled its eyes and moved its lips – or so the crowds of devotees believed. Not until the dissolution was the Cistercians' most notorious fraud uncovered: Henry VIII's commissioners found inside the rood 'certayn ingyns of old wyer with olde roten stykkes in the back of the same' and gleefully displayed their evidence of papist knavery in the market-place at Maidstone. The ill-gotten proceeds built a vast monastery; the chief remains are the pilgrims' guest-house, now a huge barn, and St Andrew's Chapel, now a cottage. At the next village along the Pilgrims' Way, the Detling Lectern, a lovely four-sided oak reading-desk on a panelled octagonal stem in St Martin's Church, presumably came from the abbey.

In the next village of Hollingbourne the old inn at the crossroads, now called the King's Head, was once known as the Pilgrims' Rest. At Harrietsham, the Pilgrims' Way passes by the church of St John the Baptist, noted for its splendid Norman font of shelly Bethersden marble – it does not follow the village High Street half a mile to the south. Old Bell Farm, which lies on the main street, is not only the best example of a sixteenth-century Wealden house close to the Pilgrims' Way, it is also the most complete example anywhere.

After Harrietsham the Pilgrims' Way climbs to the 525ft (160m) contour and passes well above Lenham, giving a good view of the A20, a later medieval road made across the Weald clay once the forests were cleared, but probably abandoned every winter for the drier chalk of the Pilgrims' Way. The huge white cross that is cut into the chalk among the grazing sheep is not a memory of pilgrimage but of the dead of two world wars. You have to descend again for the attractive old village of Charing where medieval pilgrims would have stayed at the inns or sought shelter at the third palace of the archbishops. The once stately palace courtyard is now a farmyard and the archbishop's decorated Gothic hall a barn. The gatehouse also survives from a mansion which once belonged to Thomas Becket, but its connection with Canterbury began long before the martyr's lifetime. Legend has it that Charing was given by Vortigern to the ancient English Church; even if this is not strictly accurate, it was, in fact, among the first lands bestowed on St Augustine. In the church pilgrims saw the block upon which John the Baptist was beheaded, brought back, they learned, from the Holy Land by Richard the Lionheart.

The Pilgrims' Way passes the ruins of Eastwell church and through Eastwell Park. Plantagenet's Well is close to the spot where, after the Battle of Bosworth, Richard, illegitimate son of Richard III and the last of the Plantagenet line, lived out his days in a cottage under house arrest; he was buried at Eastwell in December 1550.

Between Boughton Lees and Boughton Aluph the North Downs Way divides to form a loop around eastern Kent. Its marked path to Canterbury now largely follows the Pilgrims' Way down the Great Stour Valley. The Pilgrims' Way takes the walker straight into Boughton Aluph churchyard, a lonely site on the Downs echoed by a quaint

In the graveyard of the ruined church at Eastwell is this tomb, supposedly that of the last of the Plantagenet line, Richard, illegitimate son of Richard III

thirteenth-century church. The pilgrims probably gathered in the porch until a sufficiently large number was assembled to brave the robbers who awaited them in King's Wood.

In Chilham Park the ancient right of way has been extinguished for the fourth time. The course of the Pilgrims' Way is nevertheless clear, leading straight down to the castle, and in their guides both Hilaire Belloc and Seán Jennett covertly recommend trespassing. Chilham has in its time been a Roman camp, a Saxon castle that held out against the Danes, and a Norman keep, which remains next to a fine Jacobean manor house. Outside the park gates is the perfect English village and a pub, the White Horse, which dates back to the fifteenth century. Some miles on at the Iron Age hillfort

The Mercery: a Canterbury street in about 1250. The mule carries water for sale and the shopfronts are let down for business each day

called Bigbury Camp (TR 116577) is the reputed scene of the river battle during Caesar's second expedition, when the British chieftain Cassivelaunus so harassed five legions and two thousand cavalry that the Romans withdrew with a promise of tribute which the British, to their credit, never paid.

From this spur the Pilgrims' Way crosses the little valley to join Watling Street and Chaucer's pilgrims from London at Harbledown, which appears in the *Canterbury Tales:*

> Wist ye not where standeth a little toun
> Which that ycleped is Bob-up-and-down,
> Under the Blee in Canterbury way.

At 'Bob-up-and-down' was a leper hospital which attracted the alms and attention of pilgrims with a jewel which had once adorned Thomas Becket's shoe. Here they also glimpsed the cathedral for the first time. The golden angel on top of the central tower and the glorious shrine within may have

gone, but the majestic and awe-inspiring building still draws thousands of pilgrims every week.

Canterbury: the Hospices for Pilgrims and the Shrine of St Thomas the Martyr

The Pilgrims' Way and Watling Street enter the old city together by the West Gate, the only one of six medieval gates that remains standing. Chaucer's pilgrims stayed at the Chequer of Hope close to the cathedral, one of the inns which catered for those who were able to pay their own way. Noble and wealthy supplicants had a choice of superior lodgings, but most of them would also have had to share rooms. The poor resorted to the charities or convents such as the Hospital of St Thomas, the Poor Priests' Hospital, or the guest-houses that were run by the Franciscan, Dominican and Augustinian orders. Some remnants of these hospices survive, especially the fine Norman crypt of St Thomas. But the best place to get an idea of the medieval city is along the lane called the Mercery. Here pilgrims would have bought their essential souvenirs – lead or tin hat badges usually showing St Thomas Becket, pilgrim flasks and small flasks to carry home water mixed with holy blood. The city had much else to offer: dens where 'professional pilgrims', or tramps as we would call them, would exchange stories, and here Chaucer's Pardoner sought a low amour.

The visit to the shrine was well organised. Monks would meet the pilgrims and marshal them into orderly groups and conduct them into the cathedral through the very north transept door that had been used by both Becket and his attackers. The first station was the place where Thomas was brutally murdered, the whole scene no doubt vividly described by the practised guide, as the pilgrims kneeled on the cold flagstones and looked in horror on the tip of de Broc's sword, which had been shattered by the mighty blow that had split the martyr's skull in two. The second station was the high altar where the body lay throughout the fatal night. Finally, the pilgrims would descend to the Norman crypt and pray at the miraculous tomb itself. In 1220 the relics were translated, in a gorgeous ceremony attended by the most eminent people in the land, to a shrine behind the high altar

The shrine of Thomas Becket, Canterbury Cathedral, in about 1250

in the new Gothic cathedral. We know exactly what this shrine looked like from a detailed drawing (now in the British Library) and the thirteenth-century stained-glass window in the cathedral's miracle series. Pilgrims could still put their heads inside the shrine and kiss the actual coffin. As the drawing shows, the precious reliquary was covered by a plain cover for most of the year, but this was raised on special feast days. As the most famous shrine in the kingdom, Henry VIII's commissioners totally destroyed it at the Reformation.

Among today's tourists are numerous genuine pilgrims. Happily, the cathedral chapter have revived the old tradition of pilgrimage, and visitors, whether Christian or not, are approached by monks, nuns and lay brothers and sisters who are eager to explain the history of St Thomas and his church.

Route 7

THE PILGRIMS' WAY: WINCHESTER TO CANTERBURY

ROUTE LENGTH: 110 miles (178km) · MAPS: OS 1:50,000 Nos 178, 179, 185, 186, 187, 188, 189

PUBLIC HOUSES

Name of Pub	Location	Name of Pub	Location
Wykeham Arms***#	Winchester, Kingsgate Street	Bell****#	Godstone
Rising Sun**#	Winchester, Bridge Street	White Hart*	Godstone
Royal**#	Winchester, St Peter's Street	Clayton Arms*	Godstone
Royal Oak**	Winchester, High Street	Horns**	Otford
Cart & Horses***	King's Worthy	Bull**	Otford
Globe**	New Alresford, Broad Street	Rose & Crown*	Wrotham
Horse & Groom***	New Alresford, Broad Street/A31	George & Dragon*	Wrotham
Ship**	Bishop's Sutton	Bull***#	Wrotham
Anchor*	Ropley Dean	Vigo**	Trottiscliffe
Chequers**	Ropley	Royal Victoria & Bull**#	Rochester, High Street
Eight Bells**	Alton, Church Street	Golden Eagle**	Burham
Hen & Chicken***	Froyle, A31	Little Gem***	Aylesford
Bull***	Bentley, A31	Yew Tree**	Boxley
Nelson's Arms**	Farnham, Castle Street	King's Arms*	Boxley
Good Intent*	Puttenham	Cock Horse*	Detling
Jolly Farmer***	Puttenham	Park Gate**	Hollingbourne
Harrow***	Compton	King's Head*	Hollingbourne
Withies**	Compton	Bell**	Harrietsham
Bull's Head**	Guildford, High Street	Dog & Bear*	Lenham
Sea Horse**	Shalford	King's Head*	Charing
Percy Arms**	Chilworth	Flying Horse Inn****#	Boughton Aluph
Drummond Arms**	Albury	Woolpack***#	Chilham
White Horse***	Shere	White Horse**	Chilham
Black Horse****#	Gomshall	Falstaff**	Canterbury, North Lane
Dolphin***	Betchworth	Olde Beverlie**	Canterbury, St Stephens
Red Lion**	Betchworth	Three Tuns**	Canterbury, Watling Street

Key: ***   Highly recommended by the *Good Pub Guide*
      **   Recommended by the *Good Pub Guide*
       *   Recommended
       #   Accommodation

BED & BREAKFAST ACCOMMODATION

Map ref	Name of House	Location/Telephone number
SU 742365	Long Candovers	Hartley Mauditt, near Alton, 2 miles (3km) SE of Way. Tel: (0420) 050293
SU 820450	Trevena House Hotel	Alton Road, Farnham. Tel: (0252) 716908
TQ 172520	Burford Bridge Hotel	Westhumble, near Dorking, at A24/River Mole roundabout
TQ 724589	Carmelite Fathers	Aylesford Friary. Tel: (0622) 717272
TQ 898522	Harrow Inn	Warren Street, Lenham. Tel: (0622) 858727
TQ 930511	Three Musketeers motel	A20, between Lenham and Charing
	Ebury Hotel	New Dover Road, Canterbury. Tel: (0227) 68433

There are youth hostels at Winchester, Tanners Hatch (near Ranmore Common), Kemsing and Canterbury.

TOURIST INFORMATION OFFICES

Winchester, Farnham, Guildford, Rochester, Maidstone, Ashford, Canterbury.

8

THE MINSTER WAY

*a*ll the pilgrim routes described in this book so far have as their inspiration the fame of saints and their shrines. The pilgrimage to York Minster, however, has been inspired by the magnificent churches of the Middle Ages and the faith that built them. Perhaps you will forgive a native Yorkshireman for linking the two most famous Gothic buildings in his county: the glorious minster of St John at Beverley and the gigantic minster which dominates York so dramatically.

The shrine at York will be largely eclipsed by other themes on this route. Indeed, it is significant that no dedication ever springs to mind when we picture York Minster. Who *was* St William of York? In finding the answer, the serene architecture of the house of God becomes a mask, a mask that hides the often turbulent story of the archbishops and the naked greed and ambition of the church canons.

You might make this journey by walking along the disused railway track from Beverley to York by way of Pocklington and Market Weighton, both charming East Riding towns. It may even be possible for an athletic cyclist to follow this line by lifting his machine over fences and barbed wire. But all this is unnecessary, thanks to the energy and enthusiasm of Mr Ray Wallis of Hull. In the late 1970s he used his local knowledge to devise a beautiful 51 mile (82km) walk between our chosen monuments and he has kindly allowed us to include his 'Minster Way' here. The up-to-date Ordnance Survey maps now show where it goes, but only by a label every few miles, so to know its exact line stile by stile you may like to consult Mr Wallis' booklet *The Minster Way*, obtainable from the Lockington Publishing Co Ltd, The Studio, Railway Station, North Ferriby, telephone (0482) 633169. It is possible to mark the recommended route in detail on the Ordnance Survey simply by careful comparison with our specially drawn map,

but then a whole body of interesting local background and discussion in the booklet would be missed, as well as Mr Wallis' cheerful sense of humour.

The walk begins in the fertile plains that flank the Humber estuary, curling round through a series of delightful hamlets and villages, all of them, it seems, seldom visited for their own sakes – surely others have discovered the wonderful duck-pond at North Dalton, the picturesque church and its two old fish-ponds at Great Givendale, and the beautiful stream with its wide grassy banks dividing the village of Bishop Wilton? After roughly 20 miles (32km) the path crosses the gently rolling Yorkshire Wolds, a peaceful and pastoral scene a long way removed from the harsher beauty of the Pennines, but just as lonely. For walkers unfamiliar with the east side of Yorkshire, this is a treat, and one cunningly revealed by Mr Wallis: if you follow the Minster Way backwards the views are not as attractive.

Where the Pennines are full of bold outcrops of either millstone grit or Carboniferous limestone, the Yorkshire Wolds have a character that seems to belong to the south of England. This impression is understandable when we realise that the Yorkshire Wolds, and the Lincolnshire Wolds incidentally, are all part of the same Cretaceous chalk formation that gave prehistoric man his fine network of ridgeways in southern England. Indeed, if the Humber and the Wash were filled in again it would be possible to walk on the chalk from East Yorkshire to the Dorset coast. In the pages of this book we encounter these chalk ridgeways in the Pilgrims' Way along the North Downs, in the path to the Isle of Avalon along Grovely Ridge in Wiltshire, and in the latter part of the Green Way to Walsingham.

The soft chalk of the Wolds is worn into smooth hills like whalebacks. As with all the chalk downland, the turf may seem to be the natural ground cover, but it is in reality an artificial landscape.

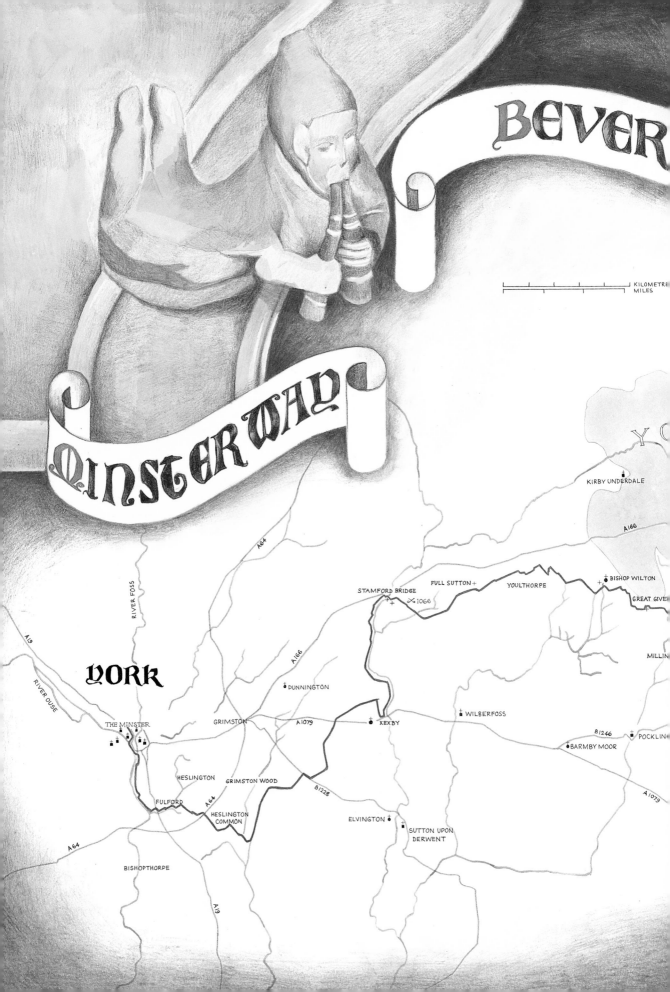

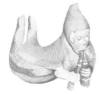

Studies of prehistoric pollen from the downland around Avebury, for instance, show that the hills had a post-glacial cover of dense oak woodland, and that, in cutting it down, neolithic man initiated catastrophic soil erosion not dissimilar to the environmental disaster now taking place in the Brazilian rain forest.

Walking westwards we cross from the Cretaceous chalk onto the older beds below it – the rock strata slope down to the east – Jurassic cement-stone, Triassic Keuper Marl, and finally Triassic Bunter sandstone with pebbly beds in the wide Vale of York. The relative thickness and hardness of the strata can result in as dramatic a scarp on the edge of the plain in East Yorkshire as any along the North Downs in Kent. Sutton Bank is popular with Yorkshire's glider pilots for its updraughts, but the scarp is not so obvious where our Minster Way leaves the chalkland near Bishop Wilton.

The approach to York is guarded by the course of the River Derwent, a tributary of the Ouse. We cross at the most historic site, Stamford Bridge (see below). To avoid busy roads and achieve a sympathetic approach to the splendours of medieval York, the path now follows the banks of the Derwent downstream to Kexby, then continues on an oblique line across country to reach the River Ouse at the village of Fulford. This detour allows walkers by far the best entry into York, some 2 miles (3km) along the towpath, beckoned always by the triple towers of the Minster that rise above the ancient city walls.

The Medieval Background and Beverley Minster
England has some large parish churches – for example, Melbourne in Derbyshire – but none is as huge as Beverley, often labelled the biggest in the country. And at Beverley it is not just the size which is impressive, for here can be seen a standard of design, of masonry and of sculpture which is far higher than at many of England's medieval cathedrals – for example, the lovely musicians that ornament the map are taken from Beverley Minster. They beg the question: why is such a splendid church in such a modest market town?

To find the answer to this question we must return to early Saxon times when England was still divided into several kingdoms. Beverley lay in the south-eastern corner of Deira, which stretched from the Humber right up to the Tweed, including the modern counties of Northumberland, Durham and Yorkshire (see Chapter 6 for the story of the kingdom's conversion to Christianity).

The eloquent, holy and learned St John of Beverley is said to have been born of noble parents at Harpham in the East Riding of Yorkshire, around the year 640. Educated at Canterbury, he became a monk at Whitby, then bishop of Hexham, and himself ordained the Venerable Bede – Bede's *History of the English Church and People* gives an account of John's life, but chiefly relates his miraculous cures. In 705 John was elected bishop of York and lived close to the church of St Michael-le-Belfry. While at York he bought some land at Beverley, extended the existing church, allowing it seven priests and seven clerks, and established close by a convent of nuns. In 718 John consecrated Wilfrid to succeed him at York and retired from his bishopric to his monastery at Beverley; he died there on 7 May 721.

Beverley's position a mere 8 miles (13km) from the Humber estuary means that John's monastery was almost certainly destroyed when the Vikings invaded in force and founded their pagan kingdom at York in 867. It seems that the refounding of a Christian community here occurred in 934, in the first generation after England was formed from the several Saxon kingdoms. In that year King Aethelstan of Wessex, himself a great collector of holy relics, travelled north to make a show of military force to the Scots and visited Beverley. The word 'minster' indicates that this was not a Benedictine monastery, but a church served by secular canons under direct royal patronage. Bede tells us that John had been buried in 'St Peter's Porch'. Presumably the local people knew where his remains were to be found, for Archbishop Aelfric of York built a costly shrine for John's bones when he was canonised in 1037, and the shrine was later rebuilt several times behind the high altar when the minster was enlarged.

The last Saxon archbishops of York marked this church out for special favour and determined to make it the major centre in the eastern part of their

The last phase in the building of Beverley Minster: Decorated Gothic style niches around the west door

province. They used their influence to heap properties, endowments and resources for building on the fortunate canons. But very little besides a font and some chevronned ornament remains even of the Norman stonework, for a disastrous fire destroyed both the town and the minster in 1188, followed by the collapse of a magnificent new tower that had been erected on slight Saxon foundations.

The chapter took full advantage of these twin disasters. Appealing for funds with the support of both king and archbishop, they built all the graceful and dignified Early English work that we see east of the nave: choir, ambulatory and four transepts. From the deeply cut mouldings and tall pointed arches, the shafts and bands of dark Frosterley marble stand out from the white magnesian limestone in a masterly display. The work was masterly indeed, for the future king's master mason, Robert de Beverley, may himself have made the design.

Looking at the damaged Norman nave, the

chapter won funds from both pilgrims to Beverley and the faithful over a wide area to rebuild it. The new work in the Decorated style, although it was started some eighty years after the choir was completed, is so carefully integrated that no abrupt change of style is obvious, inside or out – for example, the height of the triforium arcade and the pitch of the roof are the same throughout the whole length of the church. The sculptural enrichments, however, are glorious, and sensitively placed to enrich but not smother the elegant structure. Worthy of particular attention are the famous musicians in the north nave aisle, and the delicate sweetly smiling head of a queen, possibly Isabella, in the south aisle. (If it is indeed Isabella, it would be ironic, for she was responsible for the brutal murder of her husband, Edward II, at Berkeley Castle.)

The west end of Beverley Minster forms the last

phase of construction. Here the work is as well proportioned as in the rest of the building, but is more flamboyant than elsewhere, with deeply buttressed towers that soar to twice the height of the earlier roofs. On the outside the upper stages all display the fashionable Perpendicular panelling, while rows of saints in their niches enliven the lower part. Nicholas Hawksmoor, the great classical architect restored the minster in the eighteenth century, and was supposedly inspired by these western towers to design the similar pair he added to Westminster Abbey.) The stump of a tower at the central crossing now looks inadequate, but once it carried an octagonal stone lantern with a spirelet on top. Perhaps the chapter remembered how the over-ambitious Norman tower collapsed and preferred not to build such a tall one again.

The Contents of Beverley Minster

Following his canonisation, St John of Beverley's relics rested in a magnificent shrine in the ambulatory behind the high altar, the usual place for a shrine in a large medieval church. Pilgrims would have approached it along the choir aisles. When the shrine's destruction was ordered at the Reformation, the canons reburied St John in a tomb that was centrally placed at the east end of the nave.

The Percy tomb stands under the arch on the left of the high altar. The beautiful canopy is embellished with carved fruit, leaves, angels, knights and symbolic beasts, which make the monument one of the glories of medieval art. Despite its splendour, the name of the deceased has been forgotten: originally it was thought that Lady Eleanor Percy, wife of Henry de Percy of nearby Leconfield Castle, the first Lord Percy of Alnwick, was buried here, but historians now believe that the tomb was for her daughter-in-law, the Lady Idonea, who died in 1365. Like all tombs of the period, the Percy tomb would have been painted in brilliant heraldic colours.

Turning from stone to woodcarving, the choir at Beverley possesses the largest set of misericords in the British Isles – sixty-eight in all. These are the seats which, when turned up, provide a ledge for a weary monk to rest against, so allowing him to maintain the appearance of standing throughout the many services in his daily routine. The 'Ripon Carvers' made them in the early sixteenth century and the carvers' humour was often displayed in their work: in one scene a fox in friar's dress preaches to seven geese from a pulpit; in another pigs play a harp and bagpipes while the piglets dance.

The great west doors represent carving of a different school: they were made in a robust, pseudo-Gothic style by a sculptor called Thornton during Nicholas Hawksmoor's early eighteenth-century restoration. The half-baroque, half-medieval figures of the four Evangelists are a curiosity.

It is no mere whim that two Beverley musicians frame the Minster Way map, for a musical theme runs through many of the carvings in the church. Apart from the stone musicians in the north nave aisle and their caricatures in wood on the choir misericords, musicians also decorate the Percy tomb and the back of the reredos (the screen behind the high altar), while fourteenth-century angels play from their heavenly perches where the nave arches spring from the columns.

Historic Aspects of the Minster Way

In walking between the two glories of Yorkshire's medieval architecture, it would be appropriate to find other, if more modest, examples on the way. In this section we can draw attention to only one or two interesting features about each settlement, and especially its old parish church. The delightful variety of church buildings takes explorers of the area by surprise.

The walk out of Beverley is a sheer delight for anyone interested in historic buildings. A good route from the minster follows Highgate, Wednesday Market, Toll Gavel, Saturday Market (with a splendid town hall and old inns), North Bar Within and then the North Bar itself (built of brick in 1409). Beyond the line of Beverley's medieval walls we enter the wide and spacious thoroughfare called North Bar Without, which is lined with some very handsome Georgian town houses and mature horse-chestnut trees.

On the approach to the village of Scorborough the Minster Way enjoys a wide view as it follows the raised embankment of the Catchwater Drain: it

Saturday Market in Beverley has a rich collection of historic buildings: inns, this market loggia, the town hall and, rising behind, the tower of St Mary's church

resembles the Fens, especially as there is a delicate spire as a landmark. St Leonard's Church is a beautiful mid-Victorian rebuilding (1859) for the Hotham family by the architect J. L. Pearson, who was famous later in his career for designing superbly assured buildings like St Augustine's, Kilburn, and Truro Cathedral, Cornwall.

Lockington is attractive with its houses in Front Street built to face a pretty stream – an arrangement typical of East Riding villages. The gradual rise onto the Yorkshire Wolds begins here. The churchyard is full of banks and is overlooked by a Norman castle mound. Much of St Mary's Church is Norman, too: an aisleless nave, a somewhat mutilated chancel arch and a doorway. The chancel is Gothic and has a piscina and a hagioscope. There are no less than 173 painted coats-of-arms on the seventeenth-century oak panelling which lines the Estoft family chapel.

The peaceful hamlet of Kilnwick is memorable for a very high old brick wall that borders the churchyard of All Saints. Inside, an attractive Early English arcade survives, but the rest, except for a Norman north door, has been spoilt by a heavy-handed restoration.

St Andrew's, Bainton, is a fine fourteenth-century church built of millstone grit. It is, in fact, a perfect example of English church building. A Scottish army, on the rampage after defeating Edward II at the Battle of Byland in 1322, savagely destroyed the Norman church. The lavish rebuilding was due to the good fortune of the rector, William de Brocklesby, who had been a powerful and wealthy courtier. Sixteen different masons' marks can be identified, including that of the master mason of Beverley Minster. Piscinae, sedilia, stud ornament, gargoyles, a knightly tomb and niche of the Blessed Virgin – in fact, the whole gamut of glorious medieval stone carving – can be seen here.

The setting of the village of North Dalton is striking: it centres around a huge duck-pond. Around the pond stand the Star Inn and numerous trees, while above looms a huge mound, in part natural but artificially raised and now crowned by the church of All Saints. This is a clear example of how a prominent place of pagan worship was adapted to Christian use in obedience to Pope Gregory the Great's instructions to St Augustine.

The Yorkshire Wolds form the end of the chalk ridge which begins in Dorset; in this well-wooded section we are looking down to the Victorian spire of St James, Warter

The church has Norman and Early English fragments, plus a Perpendicular tower, but otherwise it all belongs to the rebuilding of 1872, under the architect J. L. Pearson. Admirers of the Pre-Raphaelite style will appreciate the stained glass in the east window which was designed by Sir Edward Burne-Jones.

The Minster Way now enters the best part of the Wolds scenery as we reach the edges of the chalk, already described in the section on the landscape. In a prominent position where once they would have been silhouetted on the skyline (SE 859539) is a group of six Bronze Age round barrows near High Barn Farm. They can be recognised now as shallow saucers in the fields. Where the path runs along the edge of the beautiful Millington Dale (SE 845528) it crosses the line of the old Roman Road from Malton (Derventio) to Brough (Petvaria) where a ferry carried the Roman army across the Humber estuary. The Roman station called

Delgovicia, mentioned in the *Antonine Itinerary* and the *Ravenna Cosmography,* is taken to lie somewhere near Millington.

The Minster Way drops down the scarp into the hamlet of Millington where there is a small Norman church with just a porch, a tiny belfry and a few medieval details. After the long walk from North Dalton, the Gate Inn is probably of more interest. Nearby, and concealed in a lovely wooded fold of the hills is Great Givendale church, which is totally isolated. The delightful little building shows some original thirteenth-century features and a spectacular Norman chancel arch, but it is mostly a highly picturesque restoration of 1849. The church has a peaceful view down its secret combe, and what appear to be two former medieval fish-ponds.

Walking up and down the Minster Way's last hill brings us near to Bishop Wilton. In the words of Ray Wallis: 'The hills are left behind now and the going is easy all the way to York, but there is still plenty of good walking to enjoy, including the banks of Bishop Wilton Beck and the rivers Derwent and Ouse.'

The earthworks in a field (SE 801554) at the top

end of the village are the foundations of a substantial medieval palace which was built in the 1240s by Walter de Grey, Archbishop of York – hence the name of the village. The settlement below the palace stretches picturesquely down either side of a grassy common or green, with the beck (a Viking word for stream used in the North) tinkling through the middle of the scene. The parish church of St Edith is the third along our route that was sympathetically restored by the architect J. L. Pearson, this time in 1856-9 for Sir Tatton Sykes, a noted jockey and racehorse owner in his day. The south doorway and chancel arch are beautiful Norman work, while the rest of the church is basically fourteenth century, including the tower and its spire, 120ft (37m) high. The stonework is of good quality, but not in the class of Bainton church. Sykes and his heirs made St Edith's something of a treasury of Victorian art – the gilded roof, the stained glass (including St John of Beverley in the west window) and, above all, the floor mosaics by Salviati, the Venetian master, a copy of a floor found in the palace of the Caesars in Rome.

St Mary's, Full Sutton, is a little church with an ivy-clad chancel and some ancient yews in the graveyard. It is a low building with a double bellcote and no tower, which was comprehensively restored in the nineteenth century to serve this hamlet. Despite a long struggle by Ray Wallis a right of way has still not been defined between Low Burtonfields Farm and Burtonfield Hall, so until it is the Minster Way follows a lane from Full Sutton to Stamford Bridge.

As every schoolchild knows, Stamford Bridge is where King Harold of England inflicted a decisive defeat on the Norwegian King Harald Hardrada in September 1066. Then came the bad news: a second invader had landed an army on the south coast. Following a forced march from Stamford Bridge, Harold met his death at Hastings just three weeks after his victory on the Derwent. Ironically, the village is now the least historic place on our route. The bonus is that Stamford Bridge has cafés, shops, four pubs and a campsite. The old corn mill beside the river has been converted to an hotel.

From Stamford Bridge to York the Minster Way follows a pleasant footpath down the right bank of the River Derwent as far as the next old bridge at Kexby. It passes the lovely hamlet of Low Catton, but the attractive group of All Saints Church and its Georgian brick rectory are out of reach on the other bank. The path zig-zags across the fields, avoiding roads and houses, until it reaches the River Ouse at Fulford – then comes the triumphant entry into York along the towpath.

The Life and Times of St William Fitzherbert
William was of noble birth, the son of Herbert, Henry I's treasurer who was sometimes called the Earl of Winchester. According to one source, William's mother was Emma, half-sister of King Stephen, but of her nothing else is known, so

This dry combe, a tributary of Millington Dale, was the Romans' preferred route through the Yorkshire Wolds

The pretty Gothic church of St Ethelburga, Great Givendale, stands at the head of an exquisite combe containing a pair of medieval fishponds

William may or may not have been a nephew of the king. At any rate he had a privileged upbringing, probably at the Norman court in Winchester. His older brother held the family estates in Yorkshire and William became treasurer and canon of York in the 1130s. His signature as a witness appears on the foundation charter of Fountains Abbey, which is ironic in view of what the Cistercians there did to him later.

When Archbishop Thurstan died in 1140, King Stephen tried to get his nephew Henry de Coilli elected, but the troublesome Henry refused the papal command to resign simultaneously as abbot of Fécamp in Normandy. Stephen then applied the royal influence in the person of the Earl of Albermarle to have his other protégé, William the treasurer, elected in his stead. Despite this pressure and, according to the Cistercians, bribery by William himself, a minority of the chapter persisted in voting for the austere Henry Murdac of Fountains Abbey.

A party of York archdeacons hurried to the king to complain about the simony and royal interference with the election, but Albermarle seized them and confined them at his castle of Bytham, Lincolnshire. In view of the dispute, the Archbishop of Canterbury refused to consecrate William. Both William and his Cistercian enemies, including St Bernard himself, appealed to Rome for settlement of the argument in their favour. Pope Innocent II hesitated for some time, but finally he declared in William's favour, as long as the Dean of York would swear that the chapter received no royal commands and William would swear on oath that he was innocent of bribery. This they did, and so, after a three-year battle, the papal legate himself consecrated William.

However, William soon showed his sluggish temperament and inability to carry out his duties – he would attend to unimportant matters while neglecting more crucial issues. In particular, when Cardinal Hincmar arrived on a mission from the new pope, Lucius II, bearing William's *pallium*, the mantle which symbolised the archbishop's office, William failed to collect it. Lucius died, and Hincmar took the pallium back to Rome, where the

new pope, Eugenius III, 'a violent Cistercian and slave of St Bernard', received fresh complaints about William. Soon the archbishop was obliged to go to Rome in person to defend his case, but to pay for the journey he sold the treasures of the church of York – thus exacerbating the case against him. Tried a second time for the same offences, he was found guilty and deposed as archbishop, after which he retired to the court in Sicily. His partisans in Yorkshire, however, took matters into their own hands when the news arrived; taking revenge on William's enemies, they burned and plundered Fountains Abbey.

With William deposed, the pope directed the chapter to proceed with a new election, but when it failed to agree, Eugenius cut short the argument by consecrating as archbishop Henry Murdac, by now Cistercian Abbot of Fountains, at Trier in Germany.

William resigned himself to his fate and went to live with his noble friends in Winchester, where he supposedly abandoned his luxurious habits in favour of prayer and study. Six years after his deposition, however, the deaths of both Bernard and Eugenius III excited his hopes anew, and, hurrying to Rome, he found his cause with the new pope, Anastasius IV, strongly aided by the timely death of Archbishop Murdac. Pitying, perhaps, William's old age and suffering, the pope gave him the pallium which he had so foolishly failed to grasp years earlier.

Proceeding in a leisurely manner to his see by way of Canterbury and his old friends at Winchester, William entered York on 9 May 1154, twelve years after his first election, to general acclaim from the populace and most of the clergy – only a hostile archdeacon called Osbert tried to bar his way to the city. According to tradition, the crowd of well-wishers was so great that the

York Minster dominates the city, especially when seen from the walls. Ghosts of the Roman ninth legion are said to haunt the cellars of the gabled Treasurer's House

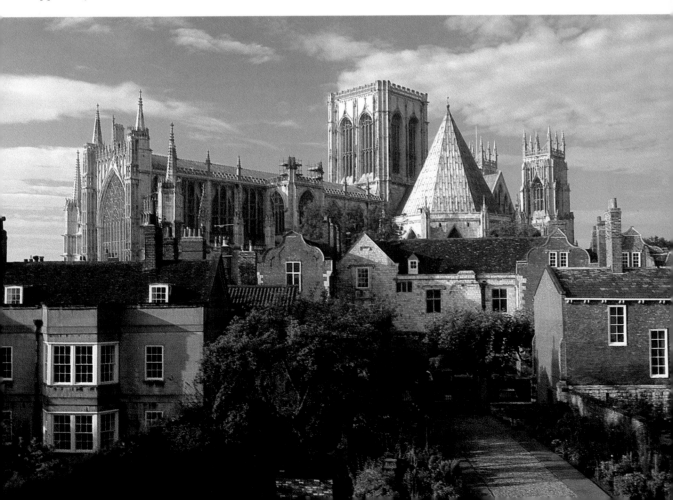

wooden bridge over the Ouse gave way, spilling hundreds of people into the water. It was William's prayer, so men thought, that saved the unfortunate people from drowning.

William immediately set about reconciling himself with the strict Yorkshire Cistercians who had so consistently opposed his wealth and laxity. In particular, he promised to restore the damage which his supporters had inflicted on Fountains Abbey. But as early as Trinity Sunday, 31 May, less than a month after his arrival, tragedy struck. The archbishop was seized with a sudden illness while celebrating Mass in his own minster. Poison was immediately suspected as the cause and antidotes were administered, but it was to no avail, for William expired eight days later. Archdeacon Osbert was accused of poisoning the eucharistic chalice.

Before long the faithful began to visit William's tomb in the minster and to hail him as a martyr. The ambitious canons at York were not slow to take up the cry, for, despite their impressive minster, they had no saint to attract pilgrims and their valuable gifts, unlike the popular nearby shrines at Beverley and Ripon. They began therefore a campaign for William's canonisation, aided by a story that holy oil had exuded from his tomb. After the customary investigations, Honorius III admitted William into the calendar of saints in 1227.

The Shrine

Fifty-six years after William's canonisation, the chapter translated the saint's mortal remains to a new shrine behind the high altar, in the presence of an exalted assembly which included Edward I. Pilgrims would have approached along the present broad choir aisles. This shrine is shown in some detail in the stained glass window dated 1422-3 in the minster's north choir aisle. However, despite the chapter's best efforts at publicity, their new saint never achieved more than local fame and the canons failed to attract the crowds they desired. Given the story of William's luxurious lifestyle and ineffectual character, coupled with the fact that only one miracle occurred during his lifetime, it is understandable that discerning pilgrims preferred to go to the shrines of holier saints.

The shrine of St William Fitzherbert in York Minster during the fourteenth century

During the Reformation parliament ordered the destruction of all the shrines in England and Wales: York's turn came in 1538, when St William's bones were re-interred in the nave. There they rested undisturbed until 1732 when a historian, Francis Drake, witnessed the discovery of a large stone coffin while workmen were relaying the floor. Drake's drawings and notes tally exactly with the coffin that was uncovered again during the major campaign to underpin the building in 1967-72. The massive sarcophagus, which was used by the sixteenth-century canons, is Roman – their forum lay directly under the present minster. The chapter has now placed the coffin and its relics in a simple shrine in the western crypt, next to the minster treasury, in a suitably Norman architectural setting of William's time.

Route 8

THE MINSTER WAY: BEVERLEY MINSTER TO YORK MINSTER

ROUTE LENGTH: 51 miles (82km) · MAPS: OS 1:50,000 Nos 105, 106, 107

PUBLIC HOUSES

Map ref	Name of Pub	Location
TA 040390	White Horse ('Nellies')***	Hengate, Beverley
TA 040390	Angel**	Butcher Row, Beverley
TA 040390	King's Head**#	Saturday Market, Beverley
TA 040390	Push**	Saturday Market, Beverley
TA 040390	Rose & Crown**#	North Bar Without, Beverley
SE 995473	Rockingham Arms*	Lockington
SE 964454	Pipe & Glass***	South Dalton, 2 miles (3km) W of path
SE 935522	Star Inn*	North Dalton
SE 830518	Gate Inn**#	Millington
SE 797552	Fleece Inn*#	Bishop Wilton
SE 710557	Three Cups**	Stamford Bridge
SE 612490	Bay Horse*	Fulford (Ouse-side York suburb)
SE 600520	Black Swan***#	Peaseholme Green, York
SE 600520	King's Arms***	King's Staithe, York (beside Ouse)
SE 600520	Olde Starre***	Stonegate, York
SE 600520	Red House**#	Stonegate, York

Key: *** Highly recommended by the *Good Pub Guide*
    ** Recommended by the *Good Pub Guide*
     * Recommended
    # Accommodation

BED & BREAKFAST ACCOMMODATION

Consult the up-to-date list supplied with copies of Ray Wallis' booklet *The Minster Way*, or consult the local tourist offices in York or Beverley. In addition, five of the recommended pubs offer overnight accommodation at the time of writing.

VILLAGES OR HAMLETS WITH GENERAL STORES

Lockington, Bainton, North Dalton, Huggate (500yd (1km) N of path), Millington, Bishop Wilton, Full Sutton, Stamford Bridge, Kexby (on the A1079, 500yd (1km) W of bridge), Fulford.

TOURIST INFORMATION OFFICES

York and Beverley.

9

THE WAY TO THE WELL

the importance of St Winefrede's Well is twofold. It is the only shrine with an unbroken record of pilgrimage from the Middle Ages to modern times – even Puritanism failed to halt the flow of pilgrims. And as a set of buildings it is the most beautiful and complete shrine, with its holy well, in the British Isles.

The way to the holy well is marked by the stones

Medieval travellers pausing at a wayside cross

of the pilgrims' road from the south, from the Roman way to Strata Florida Abbey in Cardiganshire and St David's (the route used by the Welsh) and from the border towns of Chester and Shrewsbury (the route used by ther English). If a pilgrim seeks a longer journey, these routes may be found on modern maps, but, on this occassion only, the recommended pilgrimage is a one-day walk.

The Roman road, numbered XI on the *Antonine Itinerary*, runs between the minor settlements of Varae (St Asaph) and Pentre on the Dee estuary,

St Asaph's, Britain's smallest medieval cathedral

and passes close to Holywell (not Roman) on the way. All the Welsh pilgrims would have used this road, pausing to pay their respects at St Asaph's little cathedral and shrine.

But this Roman route does not make good walking today, for it is overlain by the main North Wales trunk road, the A55(T). In only one place is the Roman road pleasant and that is a ¾ mile (1.2km) section of country lane at SJ 080752 which leads eastwards from the village of Rhuallt. The agger (or raised embankment typical of Roman roads) is often visible on deserted stretches, as at SJ 063747. But in such an agreeable part of Wales, it is possible to find a good alternative path for walkers that takes in some places of interest on the way.

Holy Wells in Britain

The cult of worship at holy wells is one which predates Christianity by many centuries all over Europe. In Britain it is closely related to Celtic rituals of nature worship, nature being obviously bountiful at springs of clear water. (The Celtic religion is explained further on p43.

Saints came to be regarded as the guardians of the sacred water in place of the pagan – that is, Celtic – water-kelpies, and other benign or malignant spirits. In this way the old gods were replaced without offending them. Of the many holy wells continuously worshipped by the natives and tolerated by the Christian priests, the following is a list of the main ones known from medieval sources: Thor's Well, Yorkshire; Beda's Well, near Jarrow; St Mary-le-Wigford, High Street, Lincoln; St Winefrede's Well, Holywell, Flintshire; St Withberga's Well, East Dereham, Norfolk; St Chad's Well, Lichfield, Staffordshire; St Edmund's Well, Oxford; St John's Well, Holywell Lane, Shoreditch, London EC2; Aquae Sulis, Bath, Avon; Woden's Well, Gloucestershire; St Gudula's Well, Gulwell; Leechwell, Totnes, and Our Lady's Well, Ladwell, all in Devon; St Agnes' Well, Chapel Porth, St Keyne's Well, and St Cleer, all in

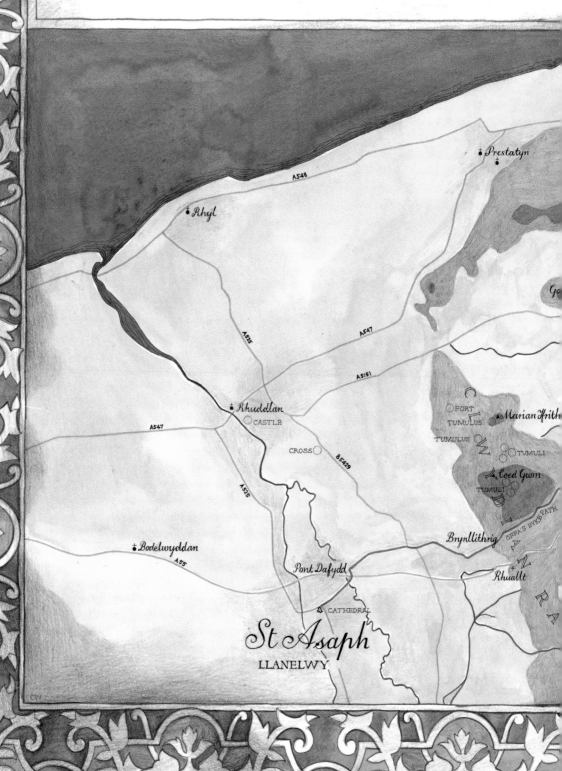

Prestatyn

Rhyl

A548

A55

A547

A5151

Go

FORT
TUMULUS
TUMULUS
TUMULI

Marian Ffrith

TUMULI

Coed Gwin

TUMULI

Rhuddlan
CASTLE

CROSS

B5429

A547

A525

Brynllithrig

ORFFA'S DYKE PATH

Bodelwyddan

A55

Pont Dafydd

Rhuallt

CATHEDRAL

St Asaph
LLANELWY

CW

HE WELL

ABBEY

TUMULI

Mostyn +

+Irelogan

Axton

OFFA'S DYKE

Sarn   TUMULI

Graig Arthur   Maen Achwyfaen   Bryn Coch

A5151   TOWER   Whitford

OFFA'S DYKE   Saith Ffynnon

ILUS   Gorsedd   Holywell
                                              ABBEY
                                 TREFFYNNON
A55
                                    CHAPEL

                        FRIARY

KILOMETRES
MILES

Brynford +

JB

Cornwall. The Rev Francis Jones' *The Holy Wells of Wales* lists over two hundred more, just in the principality. Their dense and widespread distribution is one indication of the survival of pagan customs throughout Britain. Holy wells are associated with the founding of the cathedrals at Wells, Carlisle and York, while the county score recorded by Sidney Heath is: Yorkshire, 67; Cornwall, 40; Salop, 36; Northumberland, 35; Staffordshire, 30; Cumberland, 26; Derbyshire, 36; Oxfordshire, 19; Middlesex, 16; Devon, 14; Hampshire, 11; Somerset, 11.

The best-known of the holy wells near to St Winefrede's is the famous cursing well of St Elian in Denbighshire, where, by casting a pin and a pebble into the water, a man may cause an enemy to pine away and die – to ensure that the right

The Way to the Well crosses the little Afon Clwyd by the ancient Pont Dafydd on the eastern side of St Asaph

enemy was doomed, the name of the accursed had to be inscribed upon the pebble. Also prominent among the holy wells is the Fynnon Vair at Wygfair near St Asaph, where the spring rises at the west end of the church, and is enclosed in a well of the same plan and style as that of St Winefrede.

The Smallest Cathedral in Britain: St Asaph

Our pilgrimage begins in a village, but a village elevated, like St David's, to the status of a cathedral city, for here at the Roman settlement of Varae the Celtic missionaries founded one of three early Welsh sees, called Llanelwy, meaning 'enclosure by the River Elwy'. (The third ancient cathedral is at Llandaff in Glamorgan.)

Tradition relates that in about 560 the Celtic monk St Kentigern founded the monastery and bishopric at Llanelwy while he was exiled from Strathclyde. The early benefactor was probably the noble Cadwallon Liu, whose uncle Asaph succeeded when Kentigern returned to Scotland. But the very position of the cathedral, exposed to the attacks of both Welshmen and foreigners, led to the total destruction of all early records. In 1245 and again in 1282, English troops sacked the Norman church during their conquest of Wales.

In 1143 Gilbert became the first Bishop of St Asaph to submit to consecration by the Archbishop of Canterbury, but reorganisation of the diocese in accordance with English traditions brought him and his successors into conflict with the local Welsh, as well as with the English garrison at nearby Rhuddlan Castle. To add to the clergy's problems, the population was so small that, in the reign of Edward I, the canons still had no congregation even on the great festivals.

In view of these difficult circumstances it is not surprising that it took a hundred years, with several long gaps during that period, to build even this small, squat building – only the nave has any clerestory windows, and they are just a few feet high. Nor is it puzzling that the interior has an austere and military character, for the masons of the time were probably more familiar with building castles than with building churches. Hardly was the cathedral finished when Owain Glendŵr displayed his patriotism by burning the roof during Henry

The view westwards over the Vale of Clwyd which opens out from the top of the steep scarp of the Clwydian Hills at Pen-y-mynydd, where our route follows the Offa's Dyke path

IV's dynastic struggle. However, the survival of the fine oak choir stalls and their delicate canopies lends support to the theory that a calmer period of history was reached by the late fifteenth century.

St Asaph was reputedly buried in the cathedral and his festival is celebrated each 1 May. Henry IV was, ostensibly, anxious to protect the saint's holy relics from marauders when he suggested moving the cathedral next to his powerful castle at Rhuddlan. However, no vestige of St Asaph's shrine survived Henry VIII's iconoclasm and secularisation of church property.

Since the Reformation St Asaph's cathedral has been a bastion of the Welsh language. The cathedral clergy and a lawyer called William Salusbury translated the New Testament and Book of Common Prayer into Welsh between 1550 and 1567. The entire Welsh Bible followed from the pen of William Morgan, later to become Bishop of St Asaph, who said: 'Religion, if it is not taught in the mother tongue, will lie hidden and unknown'. Victorian Protestants honoured their translators in a way that was typical of their times, by erecting a monument by public subscription. This worthy but desperately uninspired sculpture stands in the churchyard.

The Way to the Well

Starting from St Asaph, the path first crosses the Afon Clwyd (Welsh for 'Brown River'), using the ancient bridge called Pont Dafydd. Then it takes a lane eastwards towards the farm Plas yn Cwm

From the south aisle of the church of St James pilgrims can look down into the pool of St Winefrede's Well

(which simply describes its position in a valley), forking right towards Rhuallt on the footpath to join the Offa's Dyke path at Brynllithrig ('Slippery Hill') Hall. Follow the footpath north from near Pant-y-dulath to Graig-Arthur (Arthur's Rock) to reach Offa's Dyke at SJ 105790. This famous Saxon defence against the Welsh is not as prominent here as further south – look for a low bank that crosses the fields and bends to the contours.

From here a lane runs eastwards to the cross-roads at Sarn, an ancient British word meaning a road: the place-name indicates that there was a highway here long before the Celts invaded. This lane leads to the main antiquity along the route, Maen Achwyfaen ('House near the Stone': in 1858 there was a public house called the Black Horse), a tall eleventh-century wheel cross. Take a tiny lane via Bryn Coch (Red Castle) to the church and village of Whitford, then south-east to Saith Ffynnon (Seven Wells), where a footpath leads to the Victorian friary of the Franciscan order at SJ 161759, on the outskirts of the village of

Holywell. The shrine is situated down towards the sea, on a steep slope under the parish church of St James.

The Legend of St Winefrede

In the seventh century, according to myth, a young Welsh prince called Caradoc tried to seduce the virgin Winefrede. Failing in his loathsome object, but still inflamed with lust, he cut off her head 'which falling to the earth, deserved of God to have a fountain of water to spring in the place, which to this day continueth'. Winefrede's tutor, Beuno, came out of the nearby church and discovered Caradoc's evil deed. He so cursed Caradoc that the ground swallowed him up. Then, taking Winefrede's head into the church where Mass was being said, and calling on the people for their prayers, Beuno rejoined the head to the body. Not only did Winefrede miraculously revive, but she lived for another fifteen years. Her relics were revered at a shrine in Shrewsbury Abbey, some 50 miles (80km) away.

This legend was only written down by a monk in the twelfth century. In the Age of Reason, Dr William Fleetwood (1656-1723), Bishop of St

THE WAY TO THE WELL
St Asaph to St Winefrede's, Holywell

Asaph and later of Ely, 'a staunch Hanoverian and friend of Queen Anne', loathed this pilgrimage in his diocese and condemned it in the greatest detail,* declaring that he could not believe a story that had been recorded five hundred years after the saint's death. A recent Roman Catholic dictionary of saints comments rather pompously: 'Winefrede is evidently an historical personage, but equally her true story can no longer be reconstructed.'

To the student of pagan myths, on the other hand, Winefrede looks very much like the subject of Celtic legend in Christian dress. The story of a person's severed head being rejoined to his or her body which miraculously springs back to life is typical of the Celtic imagination and occurs several times in their recorded mythology.

The Shrine of St Winefrede

Margaret Beaufort, the mother of Henry VII, built the beautiful chapel and well chamber we see today in about 1490, over eight centuries after St Winefrede's death. We know nothing of the earlier buildings, although from 1240 the monks of nearby Basingwerk Abbey took care of the shrine. Henry V came here on foot from Shrewsbury in 1416 to give thanks for his successes in France; Edward IV later made the same pilgrimage. In 1427 Pope Martin V confirmed the importance of Winefrede's cult by granting the first in a series of four papal indulgences to pilgrims. The feast of Winefrede's martyrdom is celebrated on 22 June, and her natural death on 3 November.

The water flows strongly into the star-shaped well. The spacious well chamber allows pilgrims to walk all around the spring and narrow steps lead down into the water. The exquisite fan vault bears the coats-of-arms of several families connected with the cult in the late fifteenth century and supports a central boss decorated with scenes from St Winefrede's life. The water flows out of the chamber on its open side to the north and into the large rectangular bath. From there we can look back to see that the chamber forms an undercroft that supports the lovely chapel on the steep hillside above, while from inside the chapel a fine view of

the pool below may be seen from a gallery in the nave.

The unique aspect of St Winefrede's Well is the survival of the pilgrimage through the centuries of Protestant bigotry. It seems that neither the hostile events of the dissolution of the monasteries, nor the Puritan revolution in the following century, could halt the tread of faithful Catholics. In 1629, for example, a government spy reported that on St Winefrede's day between fourteen and fifteen hundred people assembled at the well with a hundred and fifty priests. The edicts and actions of monarchs, parliament, chief justices and bishops alike were unable to overcome the personal religious life and the intention to pursue it. The area was well used by Catholic recusants and elusive priests. Innkeepers preferred to pay a fine

St Winefrede's Well, Holywell, during the visit in 1688 of King James II and his Queen, Mary of Modena, to pray for a male Catholic heir

*See his *Life and Miracles of St Winefrede, together with her Litanies; and some Historical Observations made thereon* (1713).

rather than reveal the names of pilgrims to the authorities. But why the Jesuits and Bollandists chose Holywell as a focus for their activities above all the other shrines in Britain is an unanswered question.

In 1686 the stubborn and bigoted James II determined to bring his Queen, Mary of Modena, to the well to pray for a son, for he realised that his attempts to force Catholicism on an unwilling country would founder if he could not produce a Catholic heir. The royal couple presented gold rings at the shrine, as well as the shift worn by Mary Queen of Scots, the king's great-grandmother, at her execution. James' prayers were answered too late, for the Protestant revolution began shortly before the birth of his son, who became the Old Pretender.

Space prevents the inclusion of many curious details about the story of St Winefrede's Well and its cult, but the best description is a long chapter in Donald J. Hall's book *English Mediaeval Pilgrimage*.

The entrance to the parish church at Whitford, the only village visited on the short Way to the Well

Route 9

THE WAY TO THE WELL:
ST ASAPH TO ST WINEFREDE'S SHRINE

ROUTE LENGTH: 12½ miles (20km) · MAP: OS 1:50,000 No 116

PUBLIC HOUSES

Map ref	Name of Pub	Location
SJ 082730	Salusbury Arms***	Near the church, Tremeirchion, 1½ miles (2½km) S of path
SJ 182760	Royal Oak**	Greenfield Road, Holywell

Key: *** Highly recommended by the *Good Pub Guide*
 ** Recommended by the *Good Pub Guide*

BED & BREAKFAST ACCOMMODATION

Map ref	Name of House	Location/Telephone number
SJ 161760	Pantasaph Friary†	Pantasaph, 1½ miles (2½km) W of Holywell. Tel: (0352) 711053

† Retreat built in 1865 and run by the Capuchin friars.

TOURIST INFORMATION OFFICES

Prestatyn, Rhyl.

10

THE GREEN WAY

Gentle heardsman, tell to me
   Of curtesy I thee pray
Unto the towne of Walsingham
   Which is the right and ready way.

Unto the towne of Walsingham
   The way is hard for to be gon;
And verry crooked are those pathes
   For you to find out all alone.

TRADITIONAL

Pilgrims to Walsingham arrived from three directions. Those coming from the east followed the coast and have left as evidence of their traffic a medieval wayside cross on the village green at Binham half a mile from the priory there. These wayfarers would have travelled from Norwich, then England's second city in terms of population, or from the East Anglian ports. A sizable contingent would have visited the shrine of the miraculous Holy Rood of Bromholme, a fragment of the true cross which was once carried as a talisman by Count Baldwin of Flanders during the Fourth Crusade. This popular shrine was situated half a mile from the low Norfolk cliffs near Bacton.

While little remains above ground of the shrine at Bromholme, there is in a public park called The Walks at King's Lynn a rare survival of the medieval pilgrim route towards Walsingham from the west. The chapel of St Mary-on-the-Hill, better known as the Red Mount Chapel, is the most remarkable of King's Lynn's buildings, a red-brick octagonal tower containing an exquisite little cruciform chapel, which is well worth a visit if you have the chance. It was built by Robert Curraunce in 1485 especially for the use of pilgrims; the masons who crafted the famous fan vaulting in King's College Chapel, Cambridge, may have helped in its construction. After suffering a variety of demeaning uses, the citizens of King's Lynn restored it in 1828 and so preserved the most complete pilgrim chapel in England.

Most of the faithful travelled the pilgrim route from the south, along Walsingham Way, sometimes known as the Green Way. If you ask the local residents where the Way goes you will get several different answers, which has confused some investigators. The truth can be discovered by the position of the relevant pilgrim monuments, such as chapels, hospices and wayside crosses, along the Way – several intertwined roads existed along the general route through Brandon, Swaffham and Fakenham. In fact, this ancient road follows the well-drained Cretaceous chalk which rises slightly above the Cambridgeshire Fens and forms the extension into Norfolk of the prehistoric Ridgeway from Salisbury Plain. Notably its use in the Stone Age was to carry the trade with Wessex and the rest of Britain in high quality flints from the famous mine at Grime's Graves ('Odin's Workings'), where you may visit the fascinating underground galleries (TL 817899) which were excavated in the 1970s.

The pilgrims came via Ely, once almost an island in the watery Fens, where the intransigent Saxon patriot Hereward the Wake once took refuge from the fury of William the Conqueror. Since that legendary siege, the little city of Ely has stood in the background of history as men gradually drained the marshes all around. Our pilgrimage starts here because of the glorious cathedral and its touching story of St Etheldreda. But it also allows walkers to pass through three distinct landscapes: the Fens, the 'Breckland' and the fat farmland around Walsingham. From the multiple choices available the exact route recommended here is chosen by how suitable the villages and towns are for visits by modern pilgrims walking to Walsingham. We therefore avoid such places as Mundford,

The Early English lancets in the chapel of St Etheldreda, who founded Ely Cathedral in AD673

WESTMOOR FEN

FODDER FEN

B1411 A10 BURNT FEN A1101

RIVER GREAT OUSE

FELTWELL B1386

DIDLIN

ELY B1382 MUND

WITCHFORD A142 PADNAL FEN

CATHEDRAL PRICKWILLOW DECOY FEN

BOTANY BAY HOCKWOLD CUM WILTON MEDIEVAL ABYSINE CROSS

FODDER FEN SEDGE FEN LITTLE OUSE RIVER WEETING

MIDDLE FEN A10

A142 RIVER LARK B1104

GREAT FEN B1112 GRIMES G

RIVER LARK

TURF FEN LAKENHEATH BRANDON

ISLEHAM FEN MILDENHALL FEN CUT-OFF CHANNEL A1065

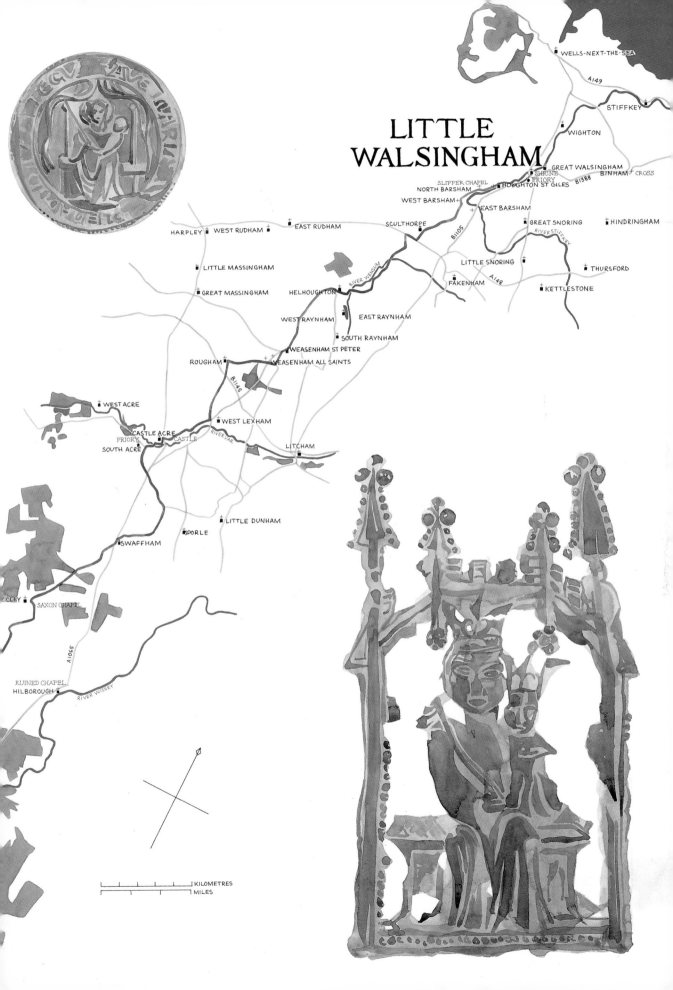

LITTLE WALSINGHAM

WELLS-NEXT-THE-SEA

A149

STIFFKEY

WIGHTON

GREAT WALSINGHAM
SHRINE   BINHAM + CROSS
SLIPPER CHAPEL   PRIORY
NORTH BARSHAM   HOUGHTON ST GILES   B1388
WEST BARSHAM +
EAST BARSHAM

HARPLEY   WEST RUDHAM   EAST RUDHAM   SCULTHORPE   GREAT SNORING   HINDRINGHAM

RIVER STIFFKEY

B1105

LITTLE MASSINGHAM   LITTLE SNORING   THURSFORD

RIVER WENSUM   A148

GREAT MASSINGHAM   HELHOUGHTON   FAKENHAM   KETTLESTONE

WEST RAYNHAM   EAST RAYNHAM

SOUTH RAYNHAM

WEASENHAM ST PETER

ROUGHAM   WEASENHAM ALL SAINTS

B1145

WEST ACRE

WEST LEXHAM

CASTLE ACRE   RIVER VAR
PRIORY   CASTLE   LITCHAM
SOUTH ACRE

LITTLE DUNHAM

SPORLE

SWAFFHAM

CLEY   SAXON CHAPEL

A1065

RUINED CHAPEL
HILBOROUGH   RIVER WISSEY

KILOMETRES

MILES

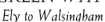

now throttled by new housing estates, and the over-modernised town centre of Fakenham, but make a point of visiting the delightful market town of Swaffham.

The Green Way's Landscape

First we encounter the Fens: low-lying marshy plains, subject to invasions of the sea, which stretch across parts of Lincolnshire, Cambridgeshire and Norfolk. In their natural state they bred a peculiar breed of 'Fenmen' who were adept at living in a watery land that was almost impenetrable on foot. In geological terms the Fens are upper Jurassic clay, but their blanket of peat and river-borne silt makes them extremely fertile. The Romans were experienced enough to recognise the usefulness of the Fenlands, and, early in their occupation of Britain, began to dig dykes for drainage and also for navigation, possibly using the defeated Iceni as forced labour. Car Dyke, their most ambitious project, stretched for 70 miles (110km) to join the River Cam near Cambridge with the River Witham at Lincoln. The lack of Roman towns and villas in the Fens may mean that the whole area was an imperial estate which was exploited to meet military needs – possibly its produce was sent by barge all the way to York.

After the departure of the Romans, the drainage system quickly fell into disrepair through lack of maintenance – as early as the fifth century the whole of the Fens had reverted to a watery waste, and it largely remained so for a thousand years. In the late eleventh century, for instance, the parishes of the Fenlands were huge and the population sparse – only eighteen people per square mile. Village communities and monasteries began dyke digging again in the twelfth century. Then work accelerated in the seventeenth century when the earls of Bedford employed Dutch engineers to construct the dead straight Old and New Bedford rivers.

Now we are left with a strange flat landscape where the eye sees mostly sky. The roads often run on banks high above the fields; the fields themselves have shrunk and settled as a result of drainage. The distances are immense and everywhere church towers may be seen. Nowhere are church towers a more important element in the landscape, which seems boundless, awe-inspiring and alien.

After the Fens comes the Breckland, an area which is totally different from the rest of Norfolk. The glaciers of prehistory left behind light sands and gravels in a depression in the underlying chalk: this porous combination and a rainfall of less than 25in (63cm) a year makes the district the driest part of the British Isles. The Breckland forest was only planted this century on the Brecks, or broken land, the home of countless rabbits. In the words of the Rev C. L. S. Linnell:

> The Breckland has changed more perhaps than any other part of Norfolk in recent years. Time was when corn grew on those lightlands and older sportsmen tell of how the last bustard was shot on Thetford Chase. But now it is mile upon mile of fir trees, for Breckland has been called upon to supply the North of England and South Wales, and – from the appearance of Brandon station – the whole world with pit props. Here and there are glimpses of old Breckland with groups of pine trees round the lovely inland meres – Langmere, Ring Mere, Thompson Water – but conifers thick and black are advancing like files of embattled troops, and the troops themselves have engulfed much of Breckland in their battle area.

It seems, however, that the reverend gentleman had an axe to grind in painting this black picture of the Breckland, for it is a relaxing area. Certainly some commercial plantations of only one species of conifer do provide such a poisonous habitat for other plants – the needles dropped on the forest floor are said to be the culprits – that the wildlife found within them is limited to the occasional deer taking shelter. But the Breckland plantations often have deciduous trees around the fringes and much wildlife within: birds, squirrels and four species of deer, as well as the rabbit which existed there before the trees. There are wide glades, small lakes or meres, and areas of cereal crops in a landscape that rolls very gently – a peaceful and empty country with only a few villages and hamlets.

Lastly comes the famous rolling farmland of north Norfolk, known as the Good Sands in con-

trast to the Breckland's bad sands. The accolade stems from the eighteenth-century transformation of the farming economy by progressive estates like Holkham and their tenants. The Cretaceous chalk of the smooth dry upland is sometimes at the surface and at others covered by sandy or loamy glacial soils. The geological difference between the Breckland and the Good Sands lies in the weight of the soil: in the Breckland it is more easily blown away. The farms are prosperous, but their fields are often too large now to please the eye.

The Story of St Etheldreda

The Venerable Bede related the life-story of the saint who founded Ely:

> Now King Egfrid took to wife Etheldreda, as was her name, the daughter of Anna, King of the East Angles, of whom we have often made mention, a man marvellously godly and in all points notable in thought and deed; which same woman had been wedded to another man, that is to say, to the Prince of the South Gyrwas [Fen countrymen], named Tondbert, before   Egfrid wedded her. But Tondbert dying a little after he took her to wife, she was given to the aforesaid king; with whom she lived twelve years and yet remained always a pure and glorious virgin.

Etheldreda finally obtained the reluctant consent of her husband to become a nun, and so was able to retreat to the island in the Fens which had been part of the dowry of her first marriage. There

> having built a monastery [in 673] she began to be a virgin mother of very many virgins dedicated to God, both in examples and lessons of heavenly life . . . She was taken to Christ in the presence of her nuns seven years after her appointment as abbess . . . Sexburga, Etheldreda's sister succeeded to the office. Sixteen years after Etheldreda's burial, this abbess decided to have her bones exhumed and transferred into the church . . . When the tomb of the holy and virginal spouse of Christ was opened and her body brought to light, it was found as free from decay as if she had died and been buried that very day.

Miracles of healing for many of those who prayed before her remains caused the great cathedral to be built over her tomb – before the Reformation her shrine was in the place of honour immediately in front of the high altar. Fragments from the base of the shrine can still be seen next to the tomb of Bishop Hugh de Northwold who extended the cathedral in her honour. The translation of her body is observed on 17 October, St Etheldreda's Fair, vulgarly called St Awdry's Fair. At one time so cheap and showy was the finery, especially lace, sold there that the contraction of 'St Awdry' gave us the English word 'tawdry'.

The marvellous cathedral rises like a huge ship above the Fens and the little buildings of this well-preserved old market town. Among all the fine English cathedrals it has a most memorable silhouette and perhaps the best setting to be found anywhere. Externally the climax is the soaring west tower with its turrets and lovely belfry, echoed inside by the delicate octagonal tower over the crossing, forming the climax internally. This is the famous Ely Octagon, which was built after the catastrophic collapse of the Norman crossing in 1322. After the catastrophe occurred the cathedral chapter called upon the services of two men of genius: their sacrist, Alan of Walsingham, and Edward III's master carpenter, William Hurley. Together they conceived a daring new space for the choir that measured 74ft (23m) across. But to roof such a span in stone was impossible, so they built the wonderful timber lantern, weighing 400 tons, which seems to float in mid-air. How this ingenious feat of architectural design was achieved is explained by an old model of the structure on show in the north transept.

Stations on the Green Way

The journey to Walsingham begins by crossing a series of railway lines, drains and navigable channels over the Fens. In the Middle Ages the largely undrained marshes were a serious barrier to travel, whereas today you may walk almost anywhere you choose in the Fens as long as you pay careful attention to where you can cross the watercourses. The hamlet of Prickwillow, reached along a track after 4½ miles (7km), is a microcosm of the

Fens: the main road looks down from an embankment onto the houses, a Victorian flint church and the surrounding land, while a bridge carries it over a tidy river used by pleasure cruisers. The scene is completed by a yellow-brick workshop dated 1842 – the drainage engine-house, now a museum with two big green diesels.

Our path crosses the Fens by a series of footpaths and tracks, striking the Little Ouse river at a spot called Botany Bay (TL 676856) and using the path along its embankments to cross over another large drain and reach the first natural slope since the Isle of Ely. This is the boundary of the Fens and Hockwold cum Wilton occupies a well-drained site at the edge of the chalk. Here we immediately find evidence of pilgrims: a medieval wayside cross stands 14ft (4m) high on the village green.

A little lane leads to the first Breckland village: Weeting was once an important place with two churches. Now you can visit its ruined castle inside a well-preserved moat, and also St Mary's, a typical Norfolk flint church. The attractive green lane that leads to the north is called Walsingham Way and once had a stone wayside cross as a guide for pilgrims. We shall now broadly follow a prehistoric track along the chalk to the Norfolk coast, and from Weeting we could make a detour to visit Grime's Graves (TL 817899), the neolithic flint mine described on p142.

We now pass through Forestry Commission fir plantations to reach Cranwich, a shrunken hamlet that preserves the oldest church on the Green Way. The site is almost certainly pre-Christian, with the unusual circular graveyard retaining the form of the pagan sanctuary. The superb Saxon tower of flints dates from 1000 and may stand on a base which is three hundred years older. The nave may also be Saxon: it now possesses later medieval windows and fortunately has been rethatched with Norfolk reed. The place feels very isolated as the wind sighs through the trees and nothing stirs at Cranwich Hall, the former parsonage, which is the only house in sight.

After crossing the River Wissey the Green Way enters the remains of the most civilised park in the Breckland. The Didlington Hall estate was one of the largest in Norfolk (it belonged to the Tyssen-Amherst family, developers of Hackney) and still boasts an ornamental lake and elaborate estate cottages, although the once huge country house has been demolished. The quality may have gone, but the geese and herons still remain to startle and

(below) Cranwich church and Saxon tower stand isolated in their circular graveyard. (opposite) River Nar: our Green Way and the Roman Peddars Way use the same ford

entrance walkers with their sudden appearance over the tree-tops at dusk. Ignore the 'Private Road' signs: fortunately no one can legally prevent an Englishman from visiting an ancient parish church, and Didlington is a gem. The stonework is mixed medieval with a Tudor roof; the Gothic fixtures – piscina, leper squint, and so on – are well carved; the exotic marble altar rail could have been bagged by an Amherst on the Grand Tour; while the spirit is echoing and evocative, for today's minute congregation, in removing the furnishings from the large nave, has partially returned the building to its medieval appearance.

In following the farm-tracks and lanes to the next village we pass the site of another wayside cross (TF 791027), marked by the Victorian Ordnance Survey, but now gone: a search with a local man out walking his dog failed to find the slightest trace. Another almost forgotten Walsingham relic lies a little to the east of here: an overgrown pilgrim chapel still stands (TF 824006) in a field, in part to a height of 15ft (5m), close to the main road through Hilborough.

Cockley Cley is another shrunken village: the parish once contained four manors and three churches. The settlement may owe its origin to the fact that it was sited directly on the prehistoric ridgeway between Grime's Graves and Hunstanton on the coast. Cockley Cley is almost unique in having the remains of two Saxon churches. We first pass St Mary's Chapel (opposite the entrance to the reconstructed village of the Iceni): the little apsed building, possibly dating from as early as 630, became a rectory in about 1550, but is now restored as a chapel. The parish church of All Saints has a round tower of flints like Cranwich, built in about 1000, possibly as a watch-tower for the surrounding Breckland, which was then much less wooded. Next to it is a splendid village pub, the Twenty Churchwardens, named after the wardens of the ten churches in the Hilborough group.

A little lane leads into Swaffham, an unspoilt Norfolk market town where the main street was made wide enough for herds of livestock and hundreds of stalls. An excellent variety of timber-framed and brick vernacular houses lines the market place, accommodating the numerous cafés and shops which keep the centre alive while the traffic goes elsewhere. A pretty spirelet that is visible for miles around guides the visitor to what is to many Swaffham's claim to fame: the church's angel roof. The beautiful double-hammerbeam construction supports a whole choir of glorious wooden angels which are delicately painted. They sing to a church which, for medieval wealth and ornament, is rivalled only in the Cotswolds. The priest's room over the vestry – also a feature of Cotswold churches – meant that the treasures could be kept under surveillance.

The Green Way leaves Swaffham by a lane that heads north-east to join the Peddars Way: this long-distance path, which broadly follows a Roman road to the north-north-west, here meanders whimsically in a style uncharacteristic of the Romans. A tiny lane leads down to a deep ford (TF 815145) with a footbridge on the River Nar, so that the Green Way enters Castle Acre by, as it were, the back door. The impressive feudal monuments in this place give the impression that ambitious plans were repeatedly unfulfilled. An eleventh-century country house was massively strengthened into a castle in 1140, but was then abandoned as early as the fourteenth century, leaving grand earthworks. The castle's thirteenth-century bailey gate is now simply a dramatic entrance to a kind of formal village green.

Castle Acre's one great success was its Cluniac priory, which drew to its guest-house crowds of Walsingham-bound pilgrims by exhibiting the arm of St Philip. It seemed of little consequence to pilgrims that this relic later proved to be spurious. The monastery's important remains include a magnificent gatehouse, the whole west end of the church, and the prior's lodging, complete with brick floors, a chimney-piece and a fancy oriel window.

The Green Way follows the right bank of the Nar but turns north before West Lexham for Rougham, a quiet hamlet full of trees, which has an old dovecote and an attractive avenue of limes. After you have crossed the main road at Weasenham All Saints, a footpath leads to Weasenham St Peter. By now it is no surprise to find that each Norfolk hamlet has a large church more fitting for a proper village. St Peter's splendid appearance was not due to the Kipton Ash sheep fair, which was once held in the parish, but to a transformation of 1870, when a much-battered and neglected building emerged as the landmark we see today.

An undulating lane leads deeper into the fat dairy farming country of north Norfolk, through Helhoughton and down the River Wensum to Shereford where the funny old flint church of St Nicholas, which leans in all directions, conceals some fine Norman detail. Another deep ford (TF 893303) with a footbridge crosses the Wensum by a pub, and takes the Green Way on to Sculthorpe. Here manor house and church enjoy an isolated feudal setting by themselves.

The hedges grow higher and greener beside the lane as we near the end of the pilgrimage via the pretty settlements of West Barsham and North Barsham. Directed by a signpost to 'OLW' (Our Lady of Walsingham), the Green Way suddenly reaches the Slipper Chapel (see p153).

England's Nazareth: the Story of the Holy House
This pilgrimage begins with a dream – a dream that had to be repeated three times to drive home its message. Although the date that the dream took place is disputed, most authorities accept the fifteenth-century version which is recorded in the *Pynson Ballad*. According to the ballad, a widowed aristocrat called Richeldis de Faverches was lady of the manor of Walsingham. The Virgin Mary came to her in a dream and took her to the house in Nazareth where the Archangel Gabriel had come to announce the birth of Jesus. Mary told Richeldis to take careful note of the measurements of the house because she wished her to build one like it in Walsingham.

The dream recurred on two other occasions, after which Richeldis ordered her builders to erect a house exactly as she had been instructed by Mary. However, when the carpenters set out the house in the water meadows on the site of the two abbey wells, the timbers refused to fit together. Richeldis remained all night in prayer seeking guidance from Our Lady and in the morning the builders found the house neatly erected on another site two hundred paces away. This miracle occurred in 1061, and bears some resemblance to the later story of the Holy House of Loreto on the Adriatic.

Nothing like the Holy House actually existed in the Holy Land in Nazareth itself the only place claimed for the annunciation by the Angel Gabriel was a cave. However, this detail did not prevent the private devotion of Richeldis becoming public property as the news of the miracle spread. A charter of about 1120 records that, on departing for Palestine, a Geoffrey de Faverches, perhaps Richeldis' son, made a gift for the foundation of a religious order to take care of the chapel, indicating that even at this early date the cult had achieved enough prominence for there to be a need for canons to look after it.

At this time the Augustinians established a large number of houses in England which blended perfectly with the special atmosphere of Walsingham. Gradually the monks rebuilt the priory on more splendid lines as pilgrims donated wealth, but the Holy House itself was inviolable and was protected by a special chapel built around it.

Royal Pilgrims

For over three hundred years Walsingham was the place of royal pilgrimage par excellence. Only one English king from the thirteen who preceded the dissolution, the transient Edward V, failed to follow the Green Way. Henry III began this royal patronage in 1226, and made many other visits. His generous gifts included sixty oak trees during the thirteenth-century rebuilding of the church. Henry's interest stimulated many other aristocrats to follow his example, including David Bruce, King of Scotland, who needed a special passport. The last royal pilgrimage, by Henry VIII, was made just five months before the king ordered the shrine's destruction.

The majority of the humble pilgrims remain unchronicled, although a selection of the various Walsingham badges they took home as souvenirs can be seen at the King's Lynn museum. We know, however, of the inns in the town where they stayed from an old account: le Beere, the White Horse, the Crownyd Lyon, the Mone and Sterr, the Cock, the Sarassyns Hede, the Swan, the Ram, the Bull, the Chekker, the Bolt and Tonn, the White Hart, the Madynhede, the Gryffon, the Bell, the Crane and the George.

Descriptions by William of Worcester and Erasmus

We know a little of what the shrine at Walsingham was like in its final flowering. William of Worcester in his description dated 1479 gives us the dimensions of the Holy House as 23ft 6in (7.1m) long × 12ft 10in (3.8m) wide, and the chapel of the Virgin Mary around it as 48ft (14.6m) × 30ft (9.1m) internally. Erasmus described the shrine as it was in about 1511:

> Within the church which I have called unfinished [it is thought that the windows were being reglazed at the time] is a small chapel, made of wainscot, and admitting devotees on each side by a narrow little door. The light is small, indeed scarcely any but from the wax lights. A most grateful fragrance meets the nostrils ... you would say it was the mansion of the saints, so much does it glitter on all sides with jewels, gold and silver.
>
> (*Colloquy on Pilgrimage*, 1526)

We know from various modern excavations that a chapel of these dimensions stood on the north side of the nave – that is, on the lawn to the side of the present Georgian mansion (which incorporates the monks' refectory).

Henry VIII and the Dissolution

As the dissolution approached, the canons of the Walsingham shrine were living decadently. A visitation by the Bishop of Norwich in 1504 named a number of them as riotous, while others were accused of drinking and joking in the pimp servant's house until dawn and of carousing around the town. The debauched prior himself, one Lowthe, was known to have slept with the wife of one of his servants and to keep a fool.

Curiously enough, Henry VIII was at first a keen patron of Walsingham, making an annual grant for candles in the shrine and visiting it himself, probably to pray for a male heir. His last visit to the shrine was only five months before it was destroyed in 1538. The canons tried to bribe the king's henchman, Thomas Cromwell, to spare them, but the Holy House and chapel were demolished and sold locally for building materials. The statue of Our Lady was carried off and burnt publicly together with other relics, probably at Chelsea. The last epitaph appears a month after the seizure in the king's 'Book of Payments': 'For the King's candle

This window is almost all that remains of the medieval Walsingham Priory; the shrine of the Holy House lay close at hand, but was utterly destroyed in the Reformation.

before Our Lady of Walsingham and to the priest there for his salary – Nil.' But Our Lady of Walsingham had the last word, for the king is said to have called on her at the hour of his death.

Subsequent History

Thomas Sidney, who lived in Walsingham as Master of the Leper Hospital, bought the abbey and site for £90, a small sum even in the sixteenth century, and turned it into a farm. The buildings quickly deteriorated. By 1738 nothing of the church remained, apart from the great east window which, as today, formed a splendid feature in the tastefully laid out gardens of the mansion.

The Modern Revival

We owe the revival of pilgrimage to Walsingham over the last century to two dedicated people: Charlotte Boyd (1837/8-1906) and the Rev Alfred Hope Patten (1885-1958). A mile before Walsingham at Houghton St Giles is an exquisite fourteenth-century building called the Slipper Chapel. The name probably derives from the pilgrims' custom of hanging up their shoes here and then enduring, as a penance, the pain of walking barefoot the rest of the way to the shrine. When, at the end of the nineteenth century, Charlotte Boyd first saw the Slipper Chapel, then in use as a farm, she planned to buy it and turn it into a convent for Anglican nuns. But during 1894, while the protracted legal work was in hand, she became a Roman Catholic. When restoration work was completed in 1897 the pope sanctioned the chapel's re-use and Bene-dictine monks from Downside Abbey near Bath moved in to take care of the building. Since then a pilgrimage has taken place every year. In 1934 the chapel became the official Roman Catholic national shrine of Our Lady. Huge marquees are set up to accommodate the crowds of summer visitors and the surrounding fields then take on the atmosphere of a British seaside holiday camp.

The interior of the small chapel is very plain and no candles are permitted – pilgrims light these in the Ghost Chapel nearby. Such decorative restraint and paucity of images greatly puzzled the Roman Catholic prisoners-of-war, both Germans and Italians, who were interned here during World War II. They preferred the Anglican shrine which was similar to the shrines they were used to in their own countries.

The Anglican Shrine

The rebirth of Anglican pilgrimage in the twentieth century may perhaps be traced to an artistic and spiritual revival in the Victorian Church of England called the Oxford Movement. A Sussex boy called Alfred Hope Patten fell under its influence and be-came a priest at Buxted where devotees of the Virgin Mary had erected a Lady Chapel to the exact dimensions of Richeldis' Holy House. In 1921 Hope Patten came to Walsingham and remained its vicar until his death in 1958.

Like some of the medieval saints, Hope Patten was a charismatic man – stubborn, charming and controversial, but capable of inspiring great

The building of the Anglican shrine to Our Lady of Walsingham in 1931

Modern pilgrims at the fourteenth-century Slipper Chapel, Walsingham, now the Roman Catholic national shrine of Our Lady

loyalty. He had a statue of Our Lady of Walsingham made to the pattern on the medieval abbey seal and placed in his parish church. Fired by the popular devotion it created, he acquired land close to the original Holy House in 1931. Over the next eight years the pilgrimage church was built around the new Holy House. The architects were Milner and Craze and the brickwork is of superb quality. The devotional facilities are elaborate for an Anglican church, and appear even more so in comparison with the simplicity of the Catholic pilgrimage to the Slipper Chapel. The Anglicans follow the mysteries of the rosary around fifteen separate chapels within the church and then the fourteen stations of the cross in the garden, all with the profoundest decorum.

The Holy Wells of Walsingham

The Abbey Wells: These two wells stand on the site where Richeldis de Faverches and her workmen failed to erect the Holy House. In the Middle Ages the wells were credited with healing powers, particularly for stomach complaints and headaches. They are now just wishing-wells – supplicants kneel on the flagstones between the wells and, dipping a hand into each one, make their wish before drinking water from each. The wells lie in the abbey gardens beyond the ruins of the east window and through a re-erected Norman archway.

The Anglican Well: Workmen digging the foundations for the new Anglican shrine discovered an ancient well, filled from the same source as the Abbey Wells just across the road. The clergy decided to restore the well and incorporate it in the shrine, where it is actively used by most of the hundred thousand pilgrims who come to Walsingham annually.

THE GREEN WAY: ELY TO WALSINGHAM

ROUTE LENGTH: 56 miles (90km) · MAPS: OS 1:50,000 Nos 132, 143, 144

PUBLIC HOUSES

Map ref	Name of Pub	Location
TL 540800	Lamb***#	Lynn Road, Ely
TL 540800	Cutter**	Annesdale, Ely, on the riverside
TL 783873	Great Eastern*	At level crossing, Brandon, 1/3 mile (1km) S of path
TL 805938	Crown***#	Crown Street, Mundford, 1¾ miles (3km) E of path
TF 827005	Swan**	Hilborough, 2½ miles (4km) E of path
TF 816152	Ostrich****#	Stocks Green, Castle Acre
TF 816152	George & Dragon**	Castle Acre
TF 831154	George & Dragon**	Newton, 1/3 mile (1km) E of path
TF 854223	Fox & Hounds**	Weasenham St Peter
TF 919296	Crown**#	Market Place, Fakenham, 1¾ miles (3km) E of path
TF 919296	Henry IV**#	Greenway Lane, Fakenham, 1¾ miles (3km) E of path
TF 893303	Old Mill*	River Wensum ford, N of Shereford
TF 916338	White Horse**	East Barsham, 1/3 mile (1km) E of path
TF 934368	Bull**	Shire Hall Plain, Walsingham

Key: *** Highly recommended by the *Good Pub Guide*   * Recommended
      ** Recommended by the *Good Pub Guide*   # Accommodation

BED & BREAKFAST ACCOMMODATION

Map ref	Name of House	Location/Telephone number
TL 560705	Warden's House	Lode Lane, Wicken, 5½ miles (9km) S of Ely. Tel: (0353) 720274. Host is Warden of Wicken Fen.
TF 863356	Cobblers	South Creake, 3 miles (5km) W of Walsingham. Tel: (032 879) 200.
TF 921353	Roman Catholic National Shrine of Our Lady	Slipper Chapel, near Walsingham. Tel: (032 872) 217/567.
TF 935369	Anglican Hospice	High Street, Walsingham. Tel: (032 872) 255.

VILLAGES OR HAMLETS WITH GENERAL STORES

Prickwillow, Hockwold cum Wilton, Brandon, Weeting, Mundford, Cockley Cley, Swaffham, Castle Acre, Rougham, Weasenham St Peter, Helhoughton, Sculthorpe, Little Walsingham.

TOURIST INFORMATION OFFICES

Ely, Thetford, Little Walsingham.

BIBLIOGRAPHY

GENERAL READING ON PILGRIMAGE

Anderson, R.M.C., *The Roads of England* (Ernest Benn, 1932).

Bunyan, John, *The Pilgrim's Progress* (1679).

Farmer, D.H., (ed), *The Age of Bede* translated by J.F. Webb (Penguin, 1983).

Finucane, R.C., *Miracles and Pilgrims: Popular Beliefs in Medieval England* (J.M. Dent & Sons, 1977).

Hall, Donald J., *English Mediaeval Pilgrimage* (Routledge & Kegan Paul, 1966).

Heath, Sidney, *In the Steps of the Pilgrims* (Rich & Cowan, 1950).

Hoskins, W.G., *The Making of the English Landscape* (Penguin, 1970).

Jusserand, J.J., *English Wayfaring Life in the Middle Ages* (Methuen, 1961).

Muir, Richard, *Shell Guide to Reading the Landscape* (Michael Joseph, 1981).

Severin, Tim, *The Brendan Voyage* (Hutchinson, 1978).

Wall, J.C., *Shrines of British Saints* (Methuen, 1905).

BOOKS ON THE DIFFERENT ROUTES

1 · *Away to Avalon*

Ashe, Geoffrey, *Avalonian Quest* (Book Club Associates, 1983). A model of incisiveness in the woolly field of Glastonbury studies.

Bord, Janet and Colin, *Mysterious Britain* (Paladin, 1974). Popular gazetteer of folklore in two volumes.
The Secret Country: More Mysterious Britain (Paladin, 1978).

Cunliffe, Barry, *Iron Age Communities in Britain* (Routledge & Kegan Paul, 1974). Popular account by one of archaeology's best communicators.

Green, Miranda J., *The Gods of the Celts* (A. Sutton, 1986). A lively and readable book.

Harding, D.W., *The Iron Age in Lowland Britain* (Routledge & Kegan Paul, 1974). Concentrates on the areas where the Iron Age evidence has been largely destroyed.

Piggott, Stuart, *The Druids* (Penguin, 1974). Explodes the myths.

Ross, Anne, *Pagan Celtic Britain: Studies in Iconography and Tradition* (Routledge & Kegan Paul, 1967). More scholarly treatment than Green.

2 · *The Waters of the Gap*

Blair, P. Hunter, *Roman Britain and Early England, 55BC–AD871* (Sphere Books, 1975). A narrative of the Roman occupation and Anglo-Saxon settlement.

Cunliffe, Barry, *Roman Bath Discovered* (Routledge & Kegan Paul, 1984). Splendid description of his excavations of the sacred spring and temple complex.

Henig, Martin, *Religion in Roman Britain* (Batsford, 1984).

Margary, Ivan D., *Roman Roads in Britain* (John Baker, 1967). The standard work, especially pp141-3 on the Aquae Sulis to Corinium stretch of the Fosse Way and pp478-80 on the Devil's Causeway in Northumberland.

Rodwell, W., (ed), *Temples, Churches and Religion in Roman Britain* (BAR 77, 1980). Seen from an archaeological viewpoint.

Salway, Peter, *Roman Britain* (Oxford University Press, 1981). The standard work, very readable.

Stewart, Bob, *The Waters of the Gap: the Mythology of Aquae Sulis* (Bath City Council, 1981). Intriguing account of the Celtic lore by an amateur.

Wacher, John, *The Towns of Roman Britain* (Batsford, 1975). Especially pp289-315 on Corinium (Cirencester).

Webster, Graham, *The British Celts and their Gods under Rome* (Batsford, 1986). A comprehensive account.

3 · *The Cornish Path*

Bizley, Maurice H., *The Church of St Piran, Perranzabuloe* (Perranzabuloe Parish Council, 1980). The story of the churches in the ever-shifting dunes.

Henderson, C.G., *Cornish Church Guide* (Oscar Blackford, 1925). The Cornish ecclesiologist's *vade mecum*.

Pearce, Susan, *The Kingdom of Dumnonia, AD350-1150* (Lodenek, 1978). The history of the old Cornish kingdom by a local curator.

St Aubyn, John, *St Michael's Mount: Illustrated History and Guide* (St Michael's Mount, 1978). The current guidebook.

Taylor, Thomas, *History of St Michael's Mount* (Cambridge University Press, 1932). A deeper account than the guidebook offers.

Tomlin, E.W.F., *In Search of St Piran: An Account of his Monastic Foundation at Perranzabuloe* (Lodenek, 1982). Reconstruction of the Celtic saint's life and religious community.

4 · The Road to the Isle

Johnson, Dr Samuel, *A Journey to the Western Isles of Scotland* (Oxford University Press, 1970). Includes his pilgrimage to Iona with the laird and Boswell in 1773.

MacNab, Peter, *The Isle of Mull* (David & Charles, 1970). Full-length guide to Mull.
Highways and Byways in Mull and Iona (Luath Press, 1988). The best short guide to the two islands.

Steven, Campbell R., 'Ben More of Mull', in Ken Wilson and Richard Gilbert (eds) *Classic Walks*, pp79-80 (Diadem Books, 1982). Describes Ben More through the climber's eyes.

Williams, Ronald, *The Lords of the Isles: the Clan Donald and the Early Kingdom of the Scots* (Chatto & Windus, 1984). The history of Dalriada in early medieval times.

5 · The Welsh Way

Bowen, E.G., *Saints, Seaways and Settlements in the Celtic Lands* (University of Wales Press, 1969). The best account of the Celtic church and its missionaries during Europe's Dark Age.

James, David W., *St David's and Dewisland: A Social History* (University of Wales Press, 1981). The history and traditions of the west Pembrokeshire peninsula by a local schoolmaster.

Morris, Jan, *The Matter of Wales: Epic Views of a Small Country* (Oxford University Press, 1984). Beautifully written introduction to the principality.

6 · The Path to Holy Island

Bede, the Venerable, *A History of the English Church and People* translated by Leo Sherley-Price (Penguin, 1968). Simply the most charming of all books on English history.
Life of Cuthbert translated by J.F. Webb (Penguin, 1965). Bede's eulogy of his predecessor, Lindisfarne's saint.

Blair, Peter Hunter, *Northumbria in the Days of Bede* (Victor Gollancz, 1976). The history of the kingdom which produced the Lindisfarne Gospels.

Frank, Graham, *Holy Island* (Butler & Butler, 1987). A guidebook with splendid illustrations by the late Ronald Embleton.

MacLaughlan, H., *Survey of the Eastern Branch of Watling Street* (London, 1864). Detailed survey of the Roman Devil's Causeway for His Grace the Duke of Northumberland.

7 · The Pilgrims' Way

Belloc, Hilaire, *The Old Road* (Constable, 1904). By far the merriest description, written by an incorrigible trespasser.

Cartwright, Julia, *The Pilgrims' Way from Winchester to Canterbury* (John Murray, 1911). The most beautiful book on the old road, with fine watercolours and much scholarship lightly worn.

Jennett, Seán, *The Pilgrims' Way* (Cassell, 1971). The best modern account of the pilgrimage.

Ward, H. Snowden, *The Canterbury Pilgrimages* (Adam & Charles Black, 1904). An example of Edwardian interest in this pilgrimage.

Watt, Francis, *Canterbury Pilgrims and their Ways* (Methuen, 1917). Often follows Belloc and Cartwright.

Wright, Christopher John, *A Guide to the Pilgrims' Way and the North Downs Way* (Constable, 1982). An alternative to Jennett's guide.

8 · The Minster Way

Carter, Robert A., *Yorkshire Churches* (Watmoughs, 1976). The Yorkshire ecclesiologist's *vade mecum*.

Wallis, Ray, *The Minster Way* (Lockington Publishing Co, 1980). The detailed and essential guidebook to this long-distance footpath, by its originator.

Wilson, Christopher, *The Shrines of St William of York* (York Minster, 1977). The life and cult of York's only saint.

9 · The Way to the Well

Bord, Janet and Colin, *Sacred Waters: Holy Wells and Water Lore in Britain and Ireland* (Granada, 1985). A much-needed study and gazetteer from the authors of *Mysterious Britain*.

Hall, Donald J., *English Medieval Pilgrimage* (Routledge & Kegan Paul, 1966). Pp18-44 cover the Holywell pilgrimage in depth.

Jones, Rev Francis, *The Holy Wells of Wales* (University of Wales Press, 1954). The survey which proved just how many sacred wells can be traced in the Celtic west of Britain.

Owen, Rev Elias, *Welsh Folk-Lore* (Woodall & Minshall, 1896). The standard Victorian account.

10 · The Green Way

Dymond, David, *The Norfolk Landscape* (Hodder & Stoughton, 1985). Part of a county-by-county survey of the making of the English landscape.

Erasmus, Desiderius, J.G. Nichols (ed), *Pilgrimages to St Mary of Walsingham and St Thomas of Canterbury* (John Murray, 1875). An eccentric scholar's satire.

Jones, David, *The Pilgrimage to Walsingham* (Norfolk Museums Service, 1987). A very informative illustrated leaflet.

Stephenson, Rev Colin, *Walsingham Way* (Darton, 1970). A useful book by a clergyman on the Anglican shrine.

INDEX